W9-DCO-123

Lowell Thomas'

VICTOR

THE MAN AND THE TOWN

by
Brian H. Levine

CENTURY ONE PRESS

2325 East Platte Avenue
Colorado Springs, Colorado 80909

Copyright 1982
By Brian H. Levine
All rights reserved
Library of Congress Catalogue
Card Number: 82-71575
ISBN 0-937080-07-1

Cover Photos:
Victor, Colorado circa 1901.

Lowell Thomas 1981 ©
Photograph by Rupe Welsh

Dedicated To:

Ross Levine/Anne English
Occasionally, we see the
same things.

With A Special Note of Gratitude to:

Lowell Thomas, Jr.
Electra
Mrs. Lowell Thomas
Wayne McCormick
Myron and Jacquelyn Levine
June Bradley
Charlotte Cox
Charles Brechtel
Bill Reed
Darlene Schomberg
Michael Carman
Bob Gant
Howard Cady
Gerald Dickler
Leland Feitz
Wilbur L. Hook

Introduction
by
Lowell Thomas, Jr.

In linking a biography of my father with a history of Victor, Brian Levine has undertaken a difficult task. But, to a large extent, he has succeeded admirably. Those early boyhood years high in the Rockies, the experiences he had and the people he met in the mining camps, shaped my dad's character in ways that led him almost inevitably into his multi-faceted career of world-traveler, author, lecturer, journalist, radio and TV commentator, and film producer. Brian's book tells how that came about while at the same time highlighting the history of Victor this "City of Gold."

Although my father lived on the East Coast most of his life, a requirement of his literary and broadcasting career, he was always a Westerner at heart. Every spring, beginning in the 1940s, when there wasn't a war on, dad would take his nightly newscast out west. His love of skiing in the Rockies and Sierras was one powerful reason, but the greater reason was his concern that he couldn't have a solid feeling for what was happening in America without spending part of each year in the West. Usually my mother and I would accompany him. I remember on one such trip, in 1949, we rode the rails from Colorado Springs to Victor and Cripple Creek as guests of former Colorado Governor Ralph Carr, an old pal of dad's. It was the last run over the famed Midland Terminal line before the tracks were to be torn up -- a sad occasion for Governor Carr and my father. However, as we rattled and chugged our way slowly up through spectacular gorges, Dad told me more about his early years up there than I'd ever heard before. He told about working in the Empire Mine as a mucker and then a driller; of carrying ore samples by horseback to the Victor assay office. (Horseback riding would be a favorite hobby for many years thereafter.) He told how he had to develop a quick wit to counter the brawn of most of his peers -- mind over fists; but he still got beat up more than once by mining camp "toughs".

Victor must have been an exciting place for a teenage boy. Gold fever was in the air, with fortune seekers pouring in from around the world. Dad told about bar-room brawls and an occasional gunfight and how his doctor father had to patch up those who survived. Through his father's eyes he saw the misery of disease among some of the tenderloin district's "ladies." Every day the good and evil of mankind was laid out before him, particularly once he graduated from paper delivery boy to cub reporter, then to editor of the **Victor Daily Record.** Dad told me he decided at the outset of his reporting career that he would seek out the good, the noble and the positive in his reporting, leaving the seamy side of life for others to write about. That was a decision he stuck to all of his life. It was his nature to look at the bright side, to be positive and ever the optimist. Victor and its enthusiastic people must have played a large role in the development of that trait.

As we rode the Midland up around Pike's Peak dad also told me he had been fascinated by tales of distant lands and places related by many of those colorful fortune seekers. No doubt those men and women instilled in him the urge to travel and explore -- and that he did right into his last 90th year. His remarkable ability to tell live audiences about his travels, his talent as a public speaker, must be credited largely to his father, Dr. Thomas, who trained him while still a boy to learn and to recite poetry before gatherings in Victor. But this distinctive, melodious voice came from his mother, Harriett Wagner Thomas, my grandmother. I still can hear her deep, mellow voice.

All of this is brought out in Brian Levine's book whose sales, by the way, will help support the Victor-Lowell Thomas Museum in my Dad's old home-town.

Preface

A biography of Lowell Thomas is inseparable from the history of Victor, Colorado. Both man and city were influenced by their environment. Victor's existence can be traced upon a gold production chart. Lowell Thomas' personality can be seen as a composite of people who lived within Victor's city limits. Daily events shaped both man and town. The link between the man's biography and the town's history can be found in the adventure of a human interest story.

An historical account cannot be investigated accurately taken out of the context of its time. The restoration of a man is void without the reconstruction of the atmosphere in which he lived. Not every incident in this history of Victor directly relates to the biography of Lowell Thomas. However, in order to reconstruct the atmosphere in which the man developed, it is necessary to witness the significant and insignificant which made the Victor of 1900-1912 unique. The biography of Lowell Thomas and the history of Victor are often divergent, but always complementary. Understanding the era and sensing the mood of the time helps in comprehending the man.

Victor was a center of inspiring figures, energetic events, and intriguing adventures. It nurtured Lowell Thomas' imagination and creativity. At times, the human interest stories in this book may seem irrelevant to the biography of Thomas. They are stories indicative of the place and time, and thus vital to seeing Victor as Lowell Thomas experienced it.

Lowell Thomas' Victor: a biography of a man; a history of a town; 1900-1912.

Victor as Lowell Thomas first saw it. A human wreath atop a mountain of gold. No other place in the country was as newsworthy as Victor, Colorado at the turn-of-the-century. There was no better place for a newspaperman like Lowell Thomas to grow up. **Cripple Creek District Museum**

Lowell Thomas, August, 1981. Photograph © by Rupe Welsh.

1981

"This was once one of the best known streets in the world." Lowell Thomas is standing on Victor Avenue in front of the City Bank Building. The town is Victor, Colorado--the City of Mines. It is 17 August 1981. He has come home.

Eighty-one years after Lowell Thomas first set foot on Victor Avenue, he has returned to the City of Mines on a very special visit. He is to be a guide on another of his unique adventures. He is going back into time. This high adventure will be one of human interest: a decade in the life of Lowell Thomas and the golden city of Victor.

As he walks on Victor Avenue, images of the past repaint themselves in his astute mind. He first saw this street when he was eight years old. The year was 1900. Almost twenty million dollars in gold had been mined from the Cripple Creek-Victor Mining District that year. The streets of Victor were paved in gold. And Victor Avenue was the center of it all.

Each building he passes reminds him of another story from his youth. He tells it in an entertaining style filled with humor and pathos. It is an example of his never-ending quest for the most captivating human interest story. When told by Lowell Thomas, the story becomes a legend.

The most enticing of these Victor legends, however, is Lowell Thomas himself.

Reliving Victor's golden era with him makes Victor Avenue one of the most important streets in America once more. The history of the town is one of America's greatest human interest stories. In the first decade of the twentieth century, Victor was constantly in the country's headlines. It epitomized the lore of the West. Gold attracted all America had to offer: invention, imagination, power, intrigue, freedom. The people who sought their fortunes in Victor were energetic, enterprising, eccentric, and some were infamous. There was no better place in America for Lowell Thomas to develop his special talents.

Through him, Victor's golden era is given a rebirth. Although he has circled the world innumerable times and lived thousands of different adventures, Lowell Thomas and Victor are indivisible. One lives through the other.

17 August 1981: cameras are following his every step. Microphones pick up his every word. He is a link, present's key to Victor's past and future. With his voice, he opens a door of time. Through his memories, one of the wonders of the world is given life again at the peak of its glory.

A year before Dr. Thomas first saw Victor, a fire nearly demolished the town. This 1899 disaster did not stop the people of Victor from holding onto their faith in the town. Rebuilding began immediately. By the time the Thomases moved into Victor in 1900, the town was a turn-of-the-century wonder.

Colorado Historical Society

A view of Victor's North Third Street. The Gold Coin shaft house towers over the other buildings from its location on Fourth and Diamond Avenue. The tracks of the Florence and Cripple Creek Railroad are in the foreground.

Cripple Creek District Museum

1900

The population of Victor and its surrounding settlements exceeded 17,000. Four hundred and seventy-five mines in the Cripple Creek-Victor Mining District were shipping more than one and a half million dollars in gold per month. The price of gold per troy ounce was $20.67. The city of Cripple Creek, with a population of approximately 25,000, was the financial and social center of the district. Over eighty percent of the producing gold mines were located around the city limits of Victor.

Victor was the City of Mines. The Gold Coin Mine's enormous and ornate shaft house soared upwards from brick foundations on Fourth Street and Diamond Avenue--near the center of town. At its most active, the Gold Coin produced $50,000 a month in gold. Miles of mining drifts, stopes, and winzes stretched out directly beneath the streets of Victor. These workings were not a part of the other major mines on Battle Mountain, just above the town.

6 April 1892: Lowell was born to Harriet and Harry Thomas of Woodington, Ohio. Early 1900, Cory Thomas induced his brother Harry to investigate the prospects of Victor, Colorado. Cory was already living in Victor. He was an engineer for the Portland Mines.

Victor had been platted 6 November 1893 by the Woods brothers. A disastrous fire occurred in August 1899. Twelve city blocks were destroyed and another twenty-five incurred heavy damage. The Victor Dr. Harry Thomas saw in 1900 was a modern wonder of the West. The picturesque mining camp on the southwest side of Pike's Peak 9,800 feet above sea level excited his imagination.

Pressed brick and reinforced steel had been used in the construction of the new buildings. Victor received many benefits from its golden wealth. Electric lights, street cars, telephones, and indoor plumbing were just a few of the luxuries engineered into the remodeled town. There was nothing like Victor and Cripple Creek anywhere else in the West.

Dr. Thomas was a devout anglophile. The fact that many English families had made their homes in Victor impressed him. Most of these families were related to the managerial staff of Stratton's Independence, Limited; a wealthy mine which had been purchased by the Venture Corporation of England in 1899. With the influx of the British, cricket matches, boxing, tea breaks, fish and chips, ales and stouts, darts, Queen Victoria, Rudyard Kipling, and William Shakespeare became increasingly popular. Plans for an opera house were formulating. Intellectual societies were prominent. Innovation and progress were major forces behind the whole district.

3

In late August 1900, Dr. Thomas moved his family from Kirkman, Iowa to Victor, Colorado. Lowell's first impression of the town: "...no one would ever mistake it for anything but a mining town. Wherever you looked, shaft houses rose up from the mountainsides. The Gold Coin mine dominated the downtown business district...."[1] A few yards southeast of the intersection of First Street and Diamond Avenue, the gallows frame of the Strong Mine stood high above the growing ore dumps. A little further up Battle Mountain was the fabulous mine which Winfield Scott Stratton, the most famous of the district's millionaires, staked out on 4 July 1891--the Independence. Towering even higher above the town was the Ajax Mine. There were so many mines above the Ajax that they were singularly indiscernable.

"Kirkman, Iowa, quickly faded in memory, and I came to believe that every town had more saloons and gambling halls than stores, with a red-light district--a tenderloin--only a few blocks away."[2] The saloons along Victor Avenue were plentiful. There was the very popular Fortune Club run by Harry Lang on the southwest corner of Third Street and Victor Avenue. There was the Senate Saloon at 308 Victor Avenue, Forch Brothers at 310, the Diamond Club at 313, the Peerless Club at 315, and the Crescent Club at 317. The Monarch Club was an outstanding favorite. It possessed fancy rooms for its patrons and its whiskey was sold in bottles embossed with the proprietor's name, W.S. Sexton.

There were more than forty saloons. Many sported gambling. Most were open twenty-four hours a day. They were small and sparsely equipped: a couple of tables, a dozen or so chairs, a wooden keg of beer, seven or eight bottles of whiskey, some cigars, and a single bartender. Few saloons were like the Monarch Club.

Victor had many forms of amusement to offer, especially for a young boy. Lowell was eight years old in September 1900. The Labor Day celebration at Pinnacle Park was an excellent opportunity for him to be introduced to the familial types of entertainment in the district.

Pinnacle Park was an attraction constructed by the Woods Investment Company aside the town of Cameron. It was very *modern* for a western mining camp. Located in the northeast part of the district, the park had a wide variety of entertainments: an electric merry-go-round, motion pictures, a zoo, a dancing pavilion, a baseball field, and other diversions. The park was opened in the spring of 1900.

Special trains were scheduled for holiday celebrations at the park. Electric cars ran every half hour to the settlement of Midway on Bull Hill. From that point, Golden Circle trains took the crowds to Cameron. Parades, contests, and sporting events began the day. An orchestra for dancing performed in the pavilion. The electric merry-go-round was in constant demand. Attendance usually ranged from three to seven thousand people.

Dr. Harry Thomas and Mrs. Harriet Wagner Thomas, having both been school teachers, were well aware that September was the beginning of the school year. Lowell was taken to Garfield School for registration. The school was located at the intersection of South Fifth Street and West Spicer Avenue. The third grade class already had more than its designated capacity. Lowell was enrolled in the fourth grade, and thus was always to be the youngest of his class. He was exceptionally prepared for his entrance into school. His parents had acquainted him with subjects his fellow students would not be exposed to for some time.

Harry George Thomas was never able to satisfy his own desire to learn. In 1892, the Thomases had moved to Cincinnati, Ohio so Harry Thomas could enroll in the state's medical school. He participated in medical classes for two years, and then the family moved to Kirkman, Iowa. During this period in American history, a license or diploma had not been required to practice medicine. Harry Thomas established an office, but he continued to study medicine. He took correspondence courses from the University of Nebraska. He obtained a doctorate in medicine.

"My father was the most persistent scholar I ever knew and remained so all of his life."[3] Dr. Thomas' knowledge was not limited to medicine. Literature, music, art, drama, mathematics, astronomy, philosophy, history, geology, and botany were just a few of the other subjects he was devoted to studying. Of all the arts, he thought elocution was the most mighty. "Your voice is the expression of your personality,"[4] he would often tell his son. At the age of 3, Lowell had begun to use his voice as few children ever do.

Dr. Thomas taught Lowell to speak eloquently through memorization and oration. Literary works of Shakespeare, Twain, Riley, Kipling, and Byron were some of the tools he used for practice. On one occasion at the Methodist Episcopal Church, 512 Victor Avenue, Dr. Thomas had Lowell stand at the podium and recite the entire work of **Paul Revere's Ride** by Riley. Lowell's voice gained a fine resonance and deep clarity through the years. His precise enunciation and emotional delivery made his oration highly enjoyable.

Harriet Thomas was also a scholar. She studied many of the subjects in which Harry Thomas immersed himself. Lowell's parents differed greatly on one subject--religion. She believed fervently in God and the Bible. She read the Bible aloud to Lowell, and he accompanied her to revival meetings. Harriet Thomas was not obsessed with religion. She merely thought it necessary to stay close to the church to promote one's own salvation.

Harry Thomas was more of a philosopher. He respected religion, but was inclined to believe most of its teachings were moralistic rather than historical. He held to the idea that religion was a personal practice, not a group ceremony.

Lowell was fortunate to have two excellent teachers for parents. He learned more at home than in the public schools. While in Victor, his father accumulated a library totaling some three thousand volumes. Mabel Barbee Lee stated in her book, **Cripple Creek Days,** that a student named

Lowell Thomas was always challenging her "knowledge of modern history."[5] She also related, "The Thomas bookshelves were filled with great classics such as Boswell's **Life of Johnson,** (Bunyan's) **Pilgrim's Progress,** Milton's **Paradise Lost,** Dante's **Inferno,** and many others including a little-known volume called **Das Kapital,** by a German political philosopher named Karl Marx."[6] The avenues of study were endless for Lowell.

While many people in Victor were busy spending time and money on gambling, liquor, mines, and the pursuit of becoming rich, the Thomases were occupied with obtaining and studying books. But the Thomases were not reclusive. And they certainly did not impress any anti-sociability upon their son.

Both Dr. and Mrs. Thomas were active in Victor's society. Mrs. Thomas joined the Methodist Episcopal Church and involved herself in the Epworth League and Woman's Club. Dr. Thomas was registered with the Teller County Medical Association, and played a major role in forming the New Century Club.

After Dr. Thomas had decided to remain in Victor in the summer of 1900, he established an office and small living quarters on Portland Avenue between Fourth and Fifth streets. When his family joined him, he rented a three-room frame house at 207 South Sixth Street. He ran an ad in the Victory **Daily Record** which listed his services as a physician and surgeon. He relocated his office. In the Bowen Building on the corner of Fourth Street and Victor Avenue, his office hours were 9 to 11 A.M., 2 to 4 P.M., and 7 to 8 P.M.

One of the first disagreeable aspects of a mining town the Thomases were introduced to was the *strike.* Ever since the 1894 labor war, the mere threat of a strike sent a surge of fear through the hearts of all who lived in the district. The violence and economic recession caused by such action affected everyone in the mining industry.

In late September, the Venture Corporation issued new rules for the miners working in Stratton's Independence. These regulations were designed to curb highgrading--the stealing of gold ore from rich veins in a mine. Highgrading was a popular supplement to a worker's $3.25 per eight-hour workday income. Estimates of losses ranged from $5,000 to $15,000 a month from the Independence alone. Entire businesses survived off these clandestine operations.

The new rules stated that every miner would have to submit to a strip search before leaving the mine's premises. The miners protested. Tensions increased when it was discovered that a Victor assayer was manufacturing special lunch pails expressly for the purpose of highgrading. After a great deal of deliberation, the strike was averted. The miners agreed to a bodily search as long as they could leave on "their drawers, undershirts, boots and stockings when passing from one change room to another under the observation of a watchman."*

The town was relieved. An incident such as this could easily catapult the district into another succession of walkouts, *scab* lists, and brutal battles.

No sooner had the trouble at the Independence Mine been settled then it was announced that Theodore Roosevelt would be arriving in Victor on 26 September. Nerves were aflare again. Mr. Roosevelt was campaigning for William McKinley for President of the United States. McKinley wanted to establish a permanent gold standard, and did not support any kind of bimetallic monetary system for the American economy. This position was not altogether laudable in Colorado. Most miners in Victor supported the free coinage of silver. They were also ready to vote for the leader of the pro-silver movement, William Jennings Bryan. To make matters worse, senators Lodge and Wolcott, outspoken opponents of Bryan, were to accompany Roosevelt. Rumblings of trouble were felt up and down Victor Avenue.

On the day Roosevelt arrived, thousands of people gathered at the Midland Terminal Depot at Fourth Street and Granite Avenue. Fifty members of the Republican Marching Club were in the crowd wearing Rough Rider uniforms. The Gold Coin Band was ready to play as soon as Roosevelt stepped off the train. The special cars of the Midland Terminal were forty-five minutes late.

When Roosevelt appeared at 5:15 P.M., he was greeted by cheers, music, and pro-Bryanite banners. The procession from the train traveled down Fourth Street to Victor Avenue, and then up North Third Street to Armory Hall. Throughout Roosevelt's speech at the meeting hall, "democratic hoodlums"* interrupted with threats and derisive comments. Children pushed up signs reading: "Bryan--16 to 1", "Hurrah for Bryan!", "Down with Trusts", and "Down with Teddy." With catcalls like "How about international bimetallism" and "Look at them teeth", Roosevelt was convinced to cut his speech short.

At 5:45 P.M., the procession started back to the depot. A dense fog had swept into town. Moods grew more ominous. Of the estimated three thousand people making up the crowd, half were women and children. Lowell was among them.

As the procession neared the depot, a skirmish broke out between a Republican marcher and a pro-Bryanite. Senator Wolcott intervened. He leaned out of his carriage and snapped the banner away from the pro-Bryanite. This signaled the fight to begin. The Republican Marching Club was quickly attacked. Free-coinage demonstrators charged Roosevelt. Women and children joined the fight. The Gold Coin Band continued playing patriotic tunes.

Nearing the intersection of Fourth and Granite, Roosevelt and his party jumped from their carriages and rushed to the awaiting train. The group was surrounded. Roosevelt's pince-nez was knocked from his face. He was suddenly blind to the onslaught. A zealous pro-Bryanite picked up a wood two-by-four and arced a swing in the direction of Roosevelt's head. This was where Lowell first advised a president--at least, that was how Mr. Thomas humorously told the story. Pulling on Roosevelt's coattail, Lowell told him to duck. It was actually Danny Sullivan who stopped the two-by-four from cracking Roosevelt's head open.

Safely aboard the Midland Terminal, Sullivan received a red sapphire ring as a measure of Roosevelt's gratitude. Lowell did not get an immediate reward for his part in the rescue.

Lowell's first friend in Victor was Carl Thomas, his father's brother's son. Carl was a year older, but they enjoyed many of the same amusements. Throwing rocks was one of their favorite pastimes. There were many rocks to throw and many targets to hit.

Marble games played with discarded steel ball bearings found around the shaft houses and ore mills were exciting for a time. Finding a somewhat level place to play proved to be a problem. The hills the town clung to were a dream for a boy and his sled in the snowy winter. But for marble games, the slopes of Victor made accuracy in shooting dependent on the cut of the curve rather than the straightness of the aim.

When Lowell could not find Carl, he would hike up North Seventh Street and sit upon an outcropping of boulders. From this advantageous outlook on Battle Mountain, he could see the Sangre de Cristo and Collegiate mountain ranges. They stretched out before him as far north as Wyoming and south as New Mexico. On crystal crisp winter days, the blueness of the sky contrasted sharply with the distant snow-covered peaks, inspiring Lowell with the great size of the world. He sensed the existence of distant places and yearned to know the stories of the people living there. The mountains represented adventure and mystery to him.

He realized Victor, too, had its own brand of adventure to offer. Millionaires were made within minutes of uncovering a wealthy gold vein. Thousands of dollars were lost at the roulette wheel in seconds. During the passage of a single day, Theodore Roosevelt could cause a riot, Bob Ford could be run out of town, or Carry Nation could break up a saloon. Legends were made daily. Myths were perpetually growing. The town was so special that it even had its own kind of *money*.

Joseph Lesher, in reaction to the decline of silver in Colorado, had printing plates made for his "Referendum dollars". The Denver Mint had struck the first of these coins for Lesher. The United States Government challenged Lesher's issuance of his "dollar". The plates were confiscated. Lesher was threatened with counterfeiting charges.

He brought his case to court and won the right to have his coins circulated in much the same manner as tokens. The one ounce coin - .950 fine silver - was purchased for $1.25, and then traded at establishments such as A.B. Bumstead's for groceries or other goods.

In December of 1900, Lesher put one thousand of his coins up for sale in Victor. Eight hundred were sold in five hours. The Lesher "dollar" became a symbol of the silver free-coinage movement in Colorado. Joseph

Lesher--a miner, assayer, and real estate salesman--profited little from his coins. But he was exemplary of Victor's unique character.

The Red Light Dance Hall was the unofficial center of the tenderloin district. It was located on North First Street near Victor Avenue. Children attending the Victor High School, on East Victor Avenue, had to pass by the dance hall daily. The saloon was open day and night. Children from the eighth through the twelfth grades attended the school. A five hundred signature petition was presented to the city council in December. The embarrassed parents of the school children wanted the dance hall moved.

In the petition, it was purported that the abbreviated costumes of the women adversely affected the children's morals. The proprietor of the saloon, G.M. Gregory, was given until 15 January 1901 to find a new place of business. Gregory ignored the order, biding his time until the Victor Opera House was completed. He was not about to miss out on the influx of money the theater would bring.

On the west end of the street, at 512 Victor Avenue, the Reverend L.C. Powell of the Methodist Episcopal Church encouraged attendance with newspaper ads in the Victor **Daily Record.** Powell advertised that the "best music" and "most interesting services" were held in his church. Services on Sundays were at 11 A.M. and 7:30 P.M. The Epworth League met at 6:30 P.M. Mrs. Thomas avidly attended these services with Lowell in tow. Lowell found ways to excuse himself from the services held at 7:30 P.M. on Wednesdays.

31 December: a Grand Ball and Banquet was given by the Victor Elks, Lodge No. 367. The banquet took place at the Baltimore Hotel. The Grand Ball was held at Armory Hall across the street. Dances included waltzes, two-steps, lancers, schottisches, quadrille-trilbys, and Chicago-glides. Dr. and Mrs. Thomas received an invitation for the festive New Year's Eve event from Dr. H.M. Cohen, chairman of the ball's floor committee.

While the new year was being celebrated, poisonous carbonic acid gases were rising in the John A. Logan Mine--a Stratton property on Bull Hill. Frederick Maudlin, John Connor, and three others were working on the 1,200 foot level of the mine when the gas encroached upon them. Maudlin and Connor were two hundred feet into the drift when Maudlin suddenly collapsed.

Carbonic acid gas, common in the mines in the southwestern section of the district, floated upwards when the barometric pressure was low. The gas, speculated to be remnants of the extinct volcano which had formed the gold district millions of years earlier, would displace oxygen with its nitrogen and carbon dioxide composition. Filling the lungs, it was only a matter of minutes before the brain was paralyzed. Miners were often caught by surprise.

Connor tried rescuing Maudlin, but he, too, succumbed to the gas. The other miners in the work crew escaped. They alerted a rescue team. Both

Maudlin and Connor were found dead. Frederick Maudlin lived at 219 South Sixth Street, a block away from the Thomases.

Victor Avenue was one of the most important streets in America in the first decade of the Twentieth Century. Ever since the Cripple Creek-Victor Mining District's healthy gold production contributed significantly to America's recovery from the Panic of 1893, the area attracted worldwide attention as well as investments.

Victor was a legend come to life. For centuries, Europeans had crossed the Atlantic Ocean in search of golden cities. In Victor, the treasures had been found.

Lowell Thomas, while living in Victor, could not help but be effected by the importance of the area. It attracted all kinds of people from all over the world. The vibrant atmosphere inspired his imagination. As he lived amidst its legendary history, the town became forever engrained in his adventurous soul.

$22,538,200 in gold was mined from the district in 1900, as reported by the Victor **Daily Record.**

A view of east Victor Avenue and an interurban tram. The tramway was powered by electricity. Dr. Thomas had his medical office in both buildings on the immediate right and left. The building on the right became the Central Drug Company. The building on the left became Carlton's City Bank.

Cripple Creek District Museum

1901

Over one million troy ounces of .950 fine gold had been produced in 1900. The Portland, Independence, Vindicator, Blue Bird, Golden Cycle, Wild Horse, Ajax, Strong, El Paso, American Eagle, Dr. Jackpot, Ramona, Findley, Jo Dandy, Lost King, and Gold King were the names of just a few of the district's mines. All of them were located 9,400 feet above sea level. Many were blasting towards the depth of 1,000 feet. Electricity powered equipment such as hoists, air drills, lights, water pumps, air filtration systems, and dynamite detonators. The majority of electric energy was processed from coal. Victor consumed 7,500 tons of coal per month.

16 January: the coal miners of Canon City called a strike. Ninety percent of Victor's coal came from the Canon City area. The price per ton leapt from six dollars to ten. A shipment of coal reached Victor the next day. Five hundred pounds was the maximum each customer was allowed to purchase.

The strike was settled in February.

John Hayes Hammond, England's famous mining engineer, returned to the district in early March. Every time Hammond came into Victor to inspect the Venture Corporation's property, the price of something dropped.

On Hammond's tour of the Independence Mine, he sampled the ore bodies north of the main shaft. After Hammond left Victor, the announcement of a law suit against Winfield Scott Stratton was printed in the papers. The charge: Stratton was supposed to have *salted* the Independence in 1899 with the intent to defraud the Venture Corporation of eleven million dollars--the sale price of the mine.

Few people took Hammond's allegations seriously. Since 1893, Stratton had steadily extracted $120,000 a month in gold from the Independence. Stratton's production schedule had rarely been altered. The miners who had worked the property under Stratton attested to his frugality. He had treated his mine like a bank, feeling that gold was worth more locked up in the ground than in free circulation on the surface. He could have easily gutted his mine of its millions in a matter of months.

T.A. Rickard, Colorado's state geologist in 1899, had estimated from his samplings that the mine had at least eight million dollars worth of ore exposed. Rickard's report also expected the mine to grow richer as it was further excavated. Hammond, as consulting engineer for the Venture Corporation in 1899, had advised against buying the mine.

The actual problem rested with the Venture Corporation's management of the property. Their staff did not understand the importance of calculating the grades of ore they shipped to the mills. The Independence was no less productive than it had been for Stratton. Withdrawals were not being tendered by a wise banker.

All Hammond's claims succeeded in accomplishing was the fall of the corporation's stock prices.

A boxing match was called a *smoker*. Nearly every men's organization sponsored bouts to raise funds. The Gold Coin Club put on a smoker on 19 March. The main contest was between Morgan Williams and Jack Martin. The twenty-round fistic event was cut short in the sixth. William's stunning punches were too much for Martin. One of Victor's most popular fighters, Williams played a part in the discovery of Jack Dempsey.

John E. Allen signed a deposition alleging that Sam Strong had hired him and another man to dynamite the Strong Mine in 1894. According to Allen, the lease held on the mine by William Lennox had not proven profitable to Strong. Under the cover of the 1894 labor war, Strong had arranged to destroy the part of the mine which contained Lennox's expensive machinery. Lennox had been forced to break the lease.

Sam Strong had been a lumberman before staking out the Strong Mine. By 1893, Strong had become one of the Cripple Creek-Victor mining millionaires. A man of extreme likes and dislikes, a wild drinker, and an insatiable gambler, Sam Strong was not above committing the crime he was accused of. Strong and his new wife were in Europe when Allen made his allegations. The trial would have to wait.

Victor was still expanding ten years after the gold district had been established. Two banks sat very close to each other on Victor Avenue: the Woods' First National Bank and D.H. Moffat's Bank of Victor. There were five schools and numerous meeting halls for the various societies. Four bookstores kept the literary set well-stocked. Dr. Thomas' favorite was the Ovren Book and Stationery Store, 500 Victor Avenue. The town had seven hotels: Baltimore, East Victor, Gold Coin, Manilla House, Myers House, Victoria, and Oxford. It even had two bottling works: Homer Peiffer and Company's Rocky Mountain, and Toby Brothers' Union.

There were fewer than fifteen physicians to tend a population of 17,000. The Victor area included the settlements of Elkton, Hollywood, Independence, Midway, Arequa, Portland Station, Strattonville, Altman, Strong's Camp, Cameron, Spinney Mills, Hull City, and Goldfield. Dr. Thomas was kept busy. However, he was more of a scholar than a businessman. Many of the medical deeds he performed were left monetarily unrewarded. He had a simple way of taking care of unpaid bills--he forgot about them.

Dr. Thomas' friend and associate in the medical profession was Dr. M.A. Latimer. His office was in rooms 5 and 6 of the Doyle Building, on the southwest corner of Fourth and Victor Avenue. Dr. Latimer and his family lived at 220 South Sixth Street, down the block from the Thomases. Drs. Thomas and Latimer shared many interests in and out of the medical profession. The study of the Bible was one of their favorite. Dr. Thomas often attended the Latimers' home Bible study group rather than Wednesday evening services at the Methodist Church.

Victor opened up for the Thomases in 1901. Dr. Thomas' practice gained paying clients. Mrs. Thomas involved herself in the church-based Ladies' Society. Lowell met new friends at Garfield School, some of whom he would associate with all of his life.

A new train service was ready for business near the end of March. The Colorado Springs and Cripple Creek Short Line made its first commercial run on 27 March. The Short Line came up from Colorado Springs through Cheyenne Canyon and made stops at Cameron, Goldfield, Victor, and Cripple Creek. Its road was ten miles shorter than that of the Midland Terminal, and its scenery was more spectacular. Along its rails, the train passed over forty-one trestles, through nine tunnels, and around two loops. The highest point on the train's route was Hoosier Pass--10,000 feet.

The initial run of the Short Line touched off a rate war with the Midland Terminal. Freight prices for hauling ore to Colorado City and Pueblo fell radically. When passenger services got underway on the Short Line, the rates dropped so fast they were almost nonexistent. Prices of all transported goods were reduced.

The month of April brought in a chill of human events. 1 April: a well-known bartender, Joe Templeton, died of morphine poisoning in the city jail. A doctor had been called in to examine Templeton when his craving for the drug increased to an intolerable level. Templeton had been arrested three days earlier for threatening to kill his wife for being "a woman of the town"*. He was twenty-five years old.

9 April: the wooden cribbing of the Granite Mine, holding hundreds of tons of waste rock, gave way and collapsed. The cribbing had been fifty-five feet high. The slide covered the James Smith house with rock ten feet in depth. Six people were trapped inside: James Smith, 45, his wife, 43, and four children, 4 through 19. There was only one survivor. A child, three years old, had been standing in the doorway when the rock rumbled down the slope. She was carried away by the slide. She suffered only minor cuts and bruises. The rest of the Smith family was crushed almost beyond recognition.

The district had produced over $100,000,000 in gold since it was established in 1891. There was no end in sight. The Cripple Creek-Victor Mining District had already surpassed the production records of Fairbanks and Nome, Alaska. Soon, it would overcome the records of Central City, the Klondike, and the Mother Lode of California.

One of the first hydroelectric power plants in the Rocky Mountain Region was built five and a half miles east of Victor. The Woods Investment Company finished construction on the Skaguay plant in the spring of 1901. Built on Beaver Creek, the cost of the operation was $527,000. It was designed on a gravity-water system. The plant housed four generators and two excitors. Its capability was 2,200 horsepower. Electricity from the plant was used by a wide range of businesses and private homes across the district from Victor to Gillett.

Hydroelectric plants did not interest Lowell and Carl. They were involved in their own engineering project. Cory Thomas was an engineer at the Portland Mine. He lived with his family at 317 South Fourth Street. Cory's knowledge and skills were being learned by his son. In the spring of 1901, when the ground had thawed, Carl and Lowell were busy working their own gold claim in Cory's backyard.

They dug underground shafts, drifts, and stopes. When their mine had a deep main shaft, they set up a head frame to support a small hoist. They continued digging, acting like engineers and miners through spring and summer. They never struck gold. But the experience was worth the effort. Carl Thomas matured into a professional bridge engineer for railroad firms. As for Lowell, the hard labor gave him stamina.

The boys pursued other interests when they were not working in their mine. They went on hikes in the canyons below Victor. Exploration of the unknown enticed Lowell to go far into the limestone caves which pierced the canyon walls. His wanderlust, urged on by mystery and the desire to learn, was already developing.

Late one summer day, a heavy rain fell rapidly in the canyon Lowell and Carl were exploring. They hid inside one of the limestone caverns to escape the torrent. From a distance, they could hear faint rumblings of rocks crashing against rocks. When they peered out of the cave, they saw a large wall of water flooding the canyon. As quickly as they could, they climbed up the cliffs. The wall of water rushed by, covering everything below them.

This occurrence did not stop the boys from investigating other areas in the district. There were countless abandoned mines and tunnels to search through. In one such tunnel on Squaw Mountain, in the vicinity of the Tornado Mine, Lowell set up a pirate cave. Saturday afternoons when there was nothing better to do, he would trek up the mountain to his cave, start a small fire with pine cones and discarded dynamite cases, and read an adventure-filled book. One of his most cherished was Jules Verne's **Twenty Thousand Leagues Under the Sea.**

Frank and Harry Woods owned Pinnacle Park. C. L. Arzeno was the general manager. Sam W. Vidler was director of special picnics, private parties, and dances. Vidler was also a newspaper correspondent and broadsword champion.

19 May: Pinnacle Park opened for its new season. The park had been remodeled and enlarged to accommodate its vast popularity. The full Gold Coin Band, twenty-four members, gave a grand concert at both Pinnacle

Park and the Cameron Athletic Field. There was dancing in the pavilion under the guidance of Professor G. A. Godat. In the carousel area, attractions such as wild animals, swings, mutoscopes (early Motion Pictures), and the rabbitry were enjoyed. The Cameron baseball team played Gillette at 2:30 P.M. All kinds of refreshments were served in the "modern" cafe. At night, the whole park was lit up in a beautiful electrical display.

Dr. Thomas, in his free hours, took Lowell on hikes into the mountains surrounding Victor. He taught Lowell to recognize different geological specimens and formations. He encouraged his son to identify botanical aspects of the region. Lowell learned with enthusiasm.

These hikes fostered personality traits which Lowell would possess all of his life. Hiking at elevations above 9,800 feet instilled endurance into his character. The air was thin and the paths steep. Health was a basic requirement. Besides keeping his body in shape, these educational tours kept his mind active. The multitude of things his father taught him were not easy to retain all at once. Lowell started keeping notebooks to aid his memory. Dr. Thomas' insatiable desire to learn soon manifested itself in his son.

Throughout his life, Lowell sought out knowledge. He learned that knowledge and entertainment were not at opposite ends of the universe. The medium between them was adventure. For Lowell, adventure was all around.

Summer glowed in the district. New styles of hats filled the windows of the Boston Clothing Store, Shilling's, and the May Clothing Company. There was the Alpine. The Bangkok. Panama. Milan. Rough and Ready. And Split Straw hats. Their prices ranged from twenty-five cents to two hundred dollars.

The average miner's daily pay was $3.50 for an eight-hour work shift.

News sped through Victor that Winfield Scott Stratton was arranging to pay off the back-taxes on Leadville's famous Matchless Mine. The price was twenty-five thousand dollars. Stratton did not want the silver mine for himself. He signed the deed over to Mrs. Tabor and her children on 4 July 1901--the tenth anniversary of his discovery of the Independence Mine.

The Fourth of July was considered an important occasion in Victor. Planning for the city-wide celebration was taken care of months in advance. Patriotism and spectacle made the people of Victor exuberant.

A reception at 8 A.M. for Governor Orman of Colorado initiated the events of the day. The governor was the first speaker on the stand at Fourth and Victor Avenue. 10 A.M., the mammoth parade began on East Victor Avenue. Almost every society, union, club, and organization in the district was represented in this display. Hundreds of people participated. Floats and costumes were luxurious and colorful. Sherman Bell, one of Theodore Roosevelt's Rough Riders, was Marshal of the Day. He led the procession up and down the center of Victor. Over six thousand people lined the avenue to watch.

A lengthy list of events and contests took place. The Knights of Pythias Band played on the corner of Fourth and Victor Avenue while the Gold Coin Band played at Second and Portland. Dancing was scheduled at a pavilion erected at Second and Portland. A ladies' reception was held in the Miners' Union Building on North Fourth. At 1:30 P.M., there were balloon ascensions and parachute jumps. Military matches, hose races, and other sports were contested at an arena built on Fourth and Victor. Prize shooting games were staged near the Independence Mine.

Lowell was especially interested in the burro races. Every boy in Victor wanted a burro. Lowell was no exception. Being only nine years old, he was not able to pay for his own burro. Until he was old enough to pay for the animal's feed and care, he could only watch the other boys with envy.

8 P.M., five thousand incandescents strung over the Bank Building, City Hall, the Doyle Bulding, the Gold Coin Shaft House, and the Ajax Mine lit up the streets of Victor. Illuminated balloon ascensions and parachute jumping performed by dogs began at 8:30 P.M. Immense electrical searchlights shimmered through the dark skies. A large electric fountain was lit up and carted through the streets. 9 P.M., all the lights went out and were immediately replaced with an exhilarating fireworks display.

The next day, the long-awaited broadsword battle was the major event. The duel attracted several thousand people into the special arena constructed on Fourth and Victor. The Gold Coin Band discharged a medley of martial music as Major J.A. McGuire rode into the area on a "black and fractious charger"*. Sam Vidler was mounted upon a pony he had named "Trouble".

During the battle, Vidler was judged to have won seven out of fifteen attacks. Two parries ended as draws. Vidler won the $100 prize. McGuire received a $50 consolation. The Major challenged Vidler to another duel to take place in New York for a $1,000 purse. Vidler proudly accepted, provided he had the money to travel at the appointed time.

As if the Fourth of July was not a big enough event for Victor, Theodore Roosevelt returned to the district on 9 August as Vice-President of the United States. Roosevelt and his party were enthralled with the trek on the Short Line. A long schedule had been mapped out in advance. And during this visit, there was to be no violence. The people of Victor-- whether pro-gold or pro-silver--were patriotic, and Roosevelt was the Vice-President.

At Portland Station, Roosevelt was escorted from the train and given the grand tour of the Portland mines by one of its illustrious owners, James Burns. Roosevelt was given two sacks of gold ore, and then he reboarded the train for Victor.

The Vice-President was ceremoniously escorted to the Gold Coin Club as twenty members of the Gold Coin Band played "El Captain." A luncheon was given by the upper echelon mine owners. Irving Howbert,

James Burns, Warren Woods, William Lennox, Spencer Penrose, and Harry Woods were among those sitting at the head table with Roosevelt. Sherman Bell and other former Rough Riders were seated nearby. Mayor Nelson Franklin initiated the toast to the Vice-President, and the Gold Coin Band acknowledged the cue by playing another patriotic melody.

Following the meal, a reception was held. Several thousand men, women, and children shook hands with Roosevelt. The Thomases were in the gathering. Lowell queued up in the reception line with everyone else. When his turn came to shake Roosevelt's hand, the Vice-President greeted him and gave him a sugar cube. Lowell was impressed by the politician. He took a place in line a second time. After a very long wait, he reached out to shake Roosevelt's hand once more. As their eyes came into contact, the Vice-President recognized Lowell and asked, "Does this mean you'll be voting twice at election time?"[7]

At approximately 2 P.M., carriages picked up the Roosevelt party and drove them through a short tour of Victor. Then the group was driven to the Gold Coin Shaft House built with red pressed bricks and colorful stained glass windows. Seventy-five people accompanied Roosevelt down the main shaft of the mine to its eight hundred foot level. Mr. and Mrs. Harry Woods--still dressed in their luncheon finery--performed the honor of being Mr. Roosevelt's guides.

Harry Woods pointed out the Gold Coin vein as they traveled a quarter of a mile down the drift. In one stope, Roosevelt was handed a pick and offered the chance to dig his own ore. He happily relieved himself of his hat and coat, then started to work. The $500 worth of ore he loosened from the vein was sacked and presented to him.

The party returned to the first level of the mine and rode fifteen mine cars, headed by an electric locomotive, three-quarters of a mile under Squaw Mountain to the Woods' Economic Extraction Mill in Eclipse Gulch. The Vice-President was shown a lump of gold concentrate recently extracted from Gold Coin ore worth over $20,000.

As they headed back to the Short Line Depot, a miner near the Oxford Hotel shouted out a gusty, "Hello, Teddy!" Roosevelt rose in his carriage, and with a look of pleasure on his face, saluted the miner with his broad hat.

For Lowell, the event was so invigorating that Theodore Roosevelt became his "number one hero".[8] Dr. Thomas bought his son Roosevelt's four volume history of America's westward movement, **The Winning of the West.** Lowell never came in close contact with his new hero again. However, Roosevelt's sons were to become dear friends later in his life. A relative, Franklin D. Roosevelt, would often be a guest at Thomas' Quaker Hill estate during the 1930's.

The district was still ecstatic when a blatant killing in Cripple Creek disrupted the aura. Sam Strong had come back from Europe. He quickly resumed his hard drinking and vigorous gambling. 22 August: Strong and his friends, including his father-in-law John Neville, were in the Newport Saloon, 375 Bennett Avenue. Grant Crumley ran a roulette game in the Newport. Strong had a violent hatred for Crumley.

Early in 1900, Strong and Crumley had quarreled over a gambling debt. Strong had refused to pay the $1,500 he owed Crumley. Strong claimed the roulette game Crumley was running in the National Hotel was not straight. Crumley filed suit and the court ordered Strong to pay Crumley $635.

At five in the morning on 22 August 1901, Strong was $140 ahead on Crumley's roulette wheel. Strong and his friends were making sport of an engineer named Tromback who had recently been shot in the leg. Tromback was a friend of Grant Crumley's. Crumley was upset because Strong had fired Tromback the day before from the Strong Mine. Neville asked Strong to leave the saloon with him. Strong refused. Instead, he went into a back room to talk with Sherman Crumley, the bartender at the Newport.

Grant Crumley scolded Neville for trying to make Strong leave while he was winning. Strong heard the shouting and rushed out of the back room. His revolver was cocked, but Neville prevented him from firing. Crumley was on the defensive. He reached behind the bar and pulled out a sawed-off shotgun. One shot blew the top of Strong's head off. Grant Crumley surrendered to the authorities.

Strong was buried in Denver. In his will, he left two million dollars to his new wife, and two hundred and fifty thousand dollars to each of his children.

Grant Crumley was held on fifty-thousand-dollar bond. The trial started in late October 1901. 7 November 1901: Crumley was found not guilty of murder--the killing was judged as self-defense.

Goldfield was a kindred town of Victor. Its outskirts touched upon Victor's city limits. Goldfield and its neighboring villages had over 5,000 residents. The major similarity between Goldfield and Victor was their labor sentiments. Both towns were vehemently pro-union.

Their kindred spirit was seen in the youth of the towns. A boy from Victor would quickly be accepted in a Goldfield club. But bring a boy over from Cripple Creek and the inherent rivalry could result in an unscheduled smoker. Almost anything from Cripple Creek was a target of aggression in either Goldfield or Victor. Embossed Cripple Creek bottles were convenient objects for the boys to release their frustrations upon. Sometimes the targets were much bigger.

Near the beginning of September, a late Florence and Cripple Creek train was passing through Goldfield. Without much warning it was brought to a quick stop. The conductor, "Blondy" Wilcox, thought he had seen a body on the trestle just ahead. He called out to whomever it was lying on the tracks. When he heard no reply, he assumed the man was too drunk to respond.

The incident irritated Wilcox. As conductor, he was responsible for the train's tardiness. He jumped out of the train and ran over to the drunken man. He pleaded with the prone figure to sleep it off at a boarding house. Receiving not even the slightest recognition from the drunk, Wilcox's anger got the best of him. He reached down to grab the man. As he pulled the body up with all his strength, the figure lunged forward and fell off the trestle. The body dropped thirty feet, then struck the rocks below.

Wilcox watched helplessly. Scurrying down the ravine, he rapidly discovered that he was the victim of a hoax. The body had broken up when it hit the rocks. It had been nothing more than clothes stuffed with excelsior.

Lowell, although he was not involved in this charade, was a prankster of his own kind. He was known to disrupt classes with sophomoric remarks. It was his way of attracting attention and promoting his leadership qualities. His pranks had no destructive intent, but they often got him into trouble.

Lowell's propensity to throw rocks turned to snowballs in winter. He and one of his school friends, Jay Herold, were entertaining themselves in alleys off Victor Avenue. They were throwing snowballs at people walking down the street. William Dingman was taking a stroll down the way from his billiards and cigar establishment on North Third Street. Lowell and Jay spotted him. Dingman was wearing a new black derby--a target begging to be hit. Jay let Lowell take aim. When the snowball hit, Jay was already running down the alley towards Portland Avenue.

In seconds, Dingman had Lowell by the collar and was dragging him to the city jail. Dingman was too jolly a character to file charges. He left Lowell with the sheriff until Dr. Thomas came to pick him up.

Days later, Lowell walked by Dingman's emporium. Dingman stopped him. He questioned Lowell about his father's reaction to the snowball incident. Lowell told him that he had "really caught it". Dingman was a good sport. He gave Lowell a handful of nickels and showed him the slot machines. From then on, Lowell lost many a coin in W.E. Dingman's billiards and cigar emporium.

6 September 1901 blew in on a shock wave. President McKinley had been shot at 4 P.M. in the Temple of Music at the Pan-American Exposition in Buffalo, New York. The assassin was a musician named Leon Czologsz. For a brief period, Mckinley appeared to be recovering from his wound. But on 14 September at 2:15 A.M., Mckinley died.

Patriotic Victor reacted. Memorial services were held at 2 P.M. on 19 September in Armory Hall. Similar memorials were held in the schools. In the afternoon, the school children formed a procession and marched down Victor Avenue. They were joined by the mayor, the city officers, Marshal Nuff, the post office employees, the Grand Army of the Republic, the Masons, and the Uniform Rank of the Knights of Pythias. In all, the count was at least one thousand strong. Lowell was among the school children. The march continued to the Methodist Church where another memorial service was performed.

The children of Garfield School received another unscheduled day off in September--this one under more pleasant circumstances. Smoke appeared to be wafting out the basement window of the school. The alarm sounded and the fire department responded. The children were hurriedly led out of the building. The firemen discovered that what looked like smoke was not at all the case.

Steam escaping from one of the boiler flues of the school's new heating system conjured up the image of a fire. There was nothing the fire department could do. For safety purposes, the children were dismissed from classes. As a large group of children reached Spicer Avenue, a loud cheer of delight echoed in the air. The din could be heard for blocks around, Lowell's voice being easily distinguished from the rest.

The arrival of fall heralded favorable discoveries in the mines. Winfield Scott Stratton hired men to work for him on an oath of secrecy. They were never to reveal anything about the inner workings of his mines. Yet, information inevitably ebbed out. Reports of rich veins could rarely be kept secret.

Rumors about Stratton's John A. Logan and American Eagle mines spread through Victor faster than electricity. Cross-cuts, developed as part of Stratton's "Bowl of Gold" theory, were producing very high-grade ore. Even at expenditures exceeding $50,000 a month, Stratton could not squander his treasure. But the rumors about his mines upset him. 1 October: he closed all his operations down. All men working in his mines were laid off.

For over a week, a lot of men in Victor were idle. Vicious talk about Stratton reared up. Men who had formerly worked for Stratton remembered when he had acted similarly. Stratton relented. He hired all the miners back and paid them in full for the days they had missed.

Lowell never met Stratton. The "Midas of the Rockies" was an eccentric recluse. However, Stratton's influence effected everyone in Victor. His hand was mighty. And when it moved, the district swayed with its actions. Lowell was mystified by this illusive man.

At the end of October, the report of an amazing strike in the Elkton Mine turned attentions temporarily away from Stratton. Crews were working on the seventh level south of the main shaft. Mostly low-grade ore surfaced until the "chimney vein" was located. As work centered in this area, purple talc and quartz crystals in large quantities were unearthed. Fluorides and quartz were positive indications of tellurides.

The men working in the drift sensed they were digging into something extraordinary. Next, a strike of manganese was uncovered. Digging through this, streaks of sylvanite were exposed. Sylvanite and calaverite, two of the major forms of gold-bearing telluride found in the district, became abundant. Exploring further, free gold was found. The estimated worth of the ore was placed at several thousand dollars per ton.

The wealth of the district was still increasing.

Not everything in Victor glistened. The Law and Order League of Teller County was frustrated. Twenty-eight hundred members of the organization signed a petition to close down gambling in the district forever. Gambling houses were given until 29 November to divest their establishments of any and all gaming paraphenalia. A few sporting establishments packed up everything and moved to Colorado City. Others, like W.E. Dingman and W.S. Sexton, stored their gambling equipment in back rooms in hopes of brighter days.

10 December: Lucy Phillips, an employee of the Red Light Dance Hall, committed suicide by swallowing carbolic acid. Lucy had lived in the district for five years. She was well-known in Victor. She had attempted killing herself in the past. She was twenty-four years old. Her body was taken to Dunn Undertaking, 204 Victor Avenue. The burial was delayed while a search was made for any surviving relatives.

The reason for Lucy's actions was never discovered. But her fate was familiar to the women of the tenderloin. Loss of appeal, drug addiction, dissolution, disease, and debts were part of the prostitute's life. The morbid side of the tenderloin's "high life" was often ignored by its casual patrons. Lucy Phillips had obviously felt the burdern of her unromantic life.

13 December 1901: The Thomases were pleased to welcome a new addition to their family. The baby's name was Helen. Nine and a half years after Lowell had been born, a second child had come into the family. The Christmas season could not have been happier for them.

Production of gold for the district, according to the Victor **Daily Record,** was $24,986,990.

The town of Independence was nestled between some of the highest paying mines of the district: the Independence, Portland, and Vindicator. Two thousand people had made their residences in this town in 1900. The town is completely abandoned today.   **Cripple Creek District Museum**

The Gold Coin Mine was a central fixture in Victor. It was the foundation of the Woods' mining empire. The Woods had always helped the miners. The strike of 1903-04 helped to undermine the empire's cornerstone. This interesting example of mining architecture has vanished, but the drifts of the Gold Coin stretch beneath Victor for miles.   **Cripple Creek District Museum**

1902

"Getting good--Victor has been practically without crime for some time past, the city jail having been without an inmate for ten days now. Desk Sergeant Murphy is getting lonesome and Police Magistrate Kavanagh is beginning to think that his position is a dead letter in the scheme of city government." Report from the Victor **Daily Record,** Saturday 8 February 1902.

As for Tim Kohane, owner of the Mint Saloon, business was not going so well. He decided to sell out to the Muelhausen Liquor Company. "Kohane, it is said, left the camp to avoid longer facing his importuning creditors, his Mint Saloon having proved something of a misnomer so far as making money was concerned."*

15 February: "Cripple Creek is in a hard way. Gambling had been closed again--her principal industry has been shut off for good, and the mining camp without any mines is extremely sore."*

The headlines of 25 February read, "Who Is Responsible For It?" The typeset of the characters was a full inch in length. At approximately three in the morning, five assay offices in Victor, two in Goldfield, and one in Cripple Creek were all simultaneously dynamited. The mine owners blamed the highgraders. The highgraders blamed the mine owners. And the assay office proprietors placed the blame on each other.

J.F. Davenport's office, located at the rear of Armory Hall between Second and Third streets, suffered the most extensive damage. The floor was blown to pieces and all the windows shattered. The Portland Avenue Assay Office lost its front window. J.G. Vanderwalker's Metallic Assay Office had its brick front wrecked. Minor damage occurred to the assay offices in Goldfield and Cripple Creek.

Frank Woods accused the highgraders of the deeds. Woods, usually a quiet man in public affairs, believed the highgraders were seeking revenge for getting less than fifty percent of the market value for the ore they stole. It was Woods' opinion that Victor could legitimately support only four or five assay shops. There were at least forty in town.

The $50,000 Victor Opera House had its opening exhibition on the night of the 25th. The display helped to cool tempers. All of Victor took pride in the luxuriant showing of the new theater's interior. They now had a playhouse that could compete with the one in Cripple Creek.

The dynamiting of the assay offices was left to the sheriff.

21 March: the Victor Opera House's first presentation played to a capacity audience. The Gold Coin Band performed as ladies in elegant gowns were escorted into the theater by men in fine suits. The decorations

were a composition of brilliant colors, the most predominant being red. The Woods, Cunninghams, Thomases, Latimers, Kyners were among the people in attendance.

The opera house was located on the corner of Second and Victor Avenue.

There were other shows in Victor. Evangelists placed the "sinful" town on their religious circuit. Lowell's mother took him to see Billy Sunday. That day the church was overcrowded. Everyone was tense with the expectation of the salvation of their souls. Lowell was entertained by the evangelist's dramatic performance. However, he was not fully aware of what was going on. When his mother rushed him up to the pulpit, he was under the misconception that the line had started because of "an offer of free candy."[9]

6 April 1902: Lowell was ten years old. He was soon to be in the sixth grade. The events in and around Victor were beginning to become real to his conscious mind. Battle Mountain was no longer one gigantic playground. Marble games and rock throwing were no longer major concerns.

He wanted to own a burro. His size and strength eliminated the possibility of capturing a wild burro in the hills and taming it himself. Purchasing a burro from a boy who wanted to exchange his animal for a horse held greater promise. But Lowell did not have enough money.

He decided he had to find employment. His parents were not fond of his working in the mines, although many children labored in them from the age of 10. Lowell gave some thought to becoming a newsboy.

When the **Record** ran an article about the union the newsboys had formed, Lowell was convinced. George Kyner had recently taken over the **Record** as editor and owner. Dr. and Mrs. Thomas were acquainted with the Kyners through the Methodist Church. Dr. Thomas promised Lowell he would talk to Mr. Kyner about the chance of Lowell being hired as a paper carrier.

Dr. Latimer had traveled to Idaho to look over the prospects of the Thunder Mountain Country. When he returned to Victor in April, the Thomas family was treated to stories of his adventures. The tales of the gold district beyond the "impenetrable" Woodtick Pass captivated Lowell. Harrowing stage and sled rides through snow-covered passes, Indians, Chinamen, and gold were just the ingredients to keep his imagination soaring.

The Law and Order League pursued its war against gambling throughout the month of April. M.J. Acton, proprietor of a saloon at 210 Victor Avenue, was arrested for allowing gaming in his establishment. Acton had to pay $200 on the spot or face thirty days in jail. He paid the $200.

John Christian had run a successful assay office in Victor since 1898. In 1901, he had decided he would rather manage a saloon. He bought the

Oxford. As soon as he opened his doors for business he began to lose money. With the Law and Order League constantly calling, Christian found it difficult to pay his overhead. His $2,000 savings vanished. Selling the Oxford was his only alternative. For $17--the price of a train ticket to Kentucky, Christian was happy to pass the deed of ownership to another unfortunate soul.

Gambling at smokers flourished. Morgan Williams fought Harry McCoy at the Victor Opera House. Seven hundred people purchased seats for the fight. Betting was rampant, and most of it was in favor of Williams. The bout lasted seven rounds. Williams was again the victor.

Williams had a few more years of fighting ahead of him. His record was an impressive one. But he decided to throw in the towel. Returning to Victor, he coached boxing in the gymnasium on the second floor of the City Hall. For a time, Lowell was one of his pugilists. When Williams discovered Jack Dempsey, he let all of his other fighters go to concentrate on Dempsey's training.

In August 1902, the May Clothing Company, 111-113 North Third Street, advertised a sale. Men's suits were sold for $6.95. Boy's suits dropped from $6.00 to $2.75. Men's hats were $2.15. Shirts were $0.65. At the McGee Mercantile Company, 103-105 South Fourth, California fruit cost 15¢ a can. Eight bars of laundry soap were 25¢. Linoleum sold for 65¢ per yard at Hackley Goods, 109 South Fourth. Majestic ranges cost $15 and Andrews upright folding beds went for $20. **Ladies Home Journal** had a ten cent cover price at Ovren Book and Stationery Store. The Woods' First National Bank possessed $50,000 in capital. And James E. Pepper Whiskey was a wonder at a $1.25 a bottle.

A quarter for a seat at the opera house was reasonable. The best seat cost a dollar, but even that was cheaper than a bottle of whiskey. Captain Jack Crawford brought his one-man show to Victor on 16 August. It was a sumptuous mixture of music and stories told with humor and pathos. The tales were from Crawford's adventures. He personified all the characters himself. The show was billed as "a picture play without a plot".*

Crawford's performance was the kind of entertainment Lowell enjoyed. Tales of adventure related in a witty yet educational frame kept Lowell in his chair. Far away places had the energies of his mind composing all sorts of exotic pictures.

The news of Willie Bomane's accident did not sit easy with Lowell's parents. Willie was twelve years old. He had been riding his burro along the edge of East Victor Avenue's sharply cut embankment. Suddenly, the burro stopped in its path. Willie was thrown off the animal. He fell twelve feet to the road below Victor Avenue. His injuries included a broken arm and a gashed cheek. After the doctor set his arm and placed two stitches in his cheek, Willie was sent to his home on South Second Street. Understandably, Willie showed an aversion to riding burros ever after. Lowell, on the other hand, was getting closer to buying his animal. He did not let his parents' foreboding affect him.

W.E. Dingman's cigar emporium display window caused a stir. The Uniform Rank of the Knights of Pythias had sent him $500 in new $20 gold pieces. The coins were from the San Francisco Mint. Sherman Bell and H.A. Naylor thought they would be excellent advertising for Dingman's store. A message from Victor Company No. 8 of the Knights accompanied the coins: "Some of the Gold Won by the Boys".* The "Boys" were really playing up their own good fortune.

The coins attracted so many people that Dingman displayed only a few at a time. Some feared a daring thief might break the window and steal the gold pieces. Dingman took precautions.

A couple of days after the coins arrived, Dingman received another telegram from Sherman Bell. Their train had been wrecked in Elko, Nevada. No one was hurt. The Southern Pacific supplied them with another special train. The "Boys" would be in Victor only a few hours behind schedule.

When Bell, Naylor, and the other Knights found themselves on familiar soil, they wasted no time gambling away their gold in Dingman's emporium.

August was a thunderous month. On the 23rd, Doc Birdsell was working one thousand feet below the surface in the Independence Mine. Witnesses claim they saw a big ball of flame explode around the mine's shaft house. A bolt of lightning tore through the building, followed an air pipe down two hundred feet and then another pipe for eight hundred feet. Birdsell, a machineman, was knocked down by the electric shock. Uninjured, he picked himself up and walked away from the accident.

The town of Anaconda was not as lucky as Birdsell. That same day, a thundercloud burst over the town, flooding the streets. A wash of water four feet high swept two houses and the tracks of the Florence and Cripple Creek Railroad down the mountain. No one was injured.

The new school year was about to begin. Lowell was in sixth grade. To initiate the term, Ovren Books staged a promotional contest. In the store's windows, a myriad of new school tablets had been haphazardly piled up. "Six prizes to the most successful guessers"* ran the ad. First prize was a five dollar Vive camera. Second prize--the one which interested Lowell-- was a book, **Story of the Rough Riders.** For every ten cents worth of school supplies, a child was able to offer one guess. The promotional gimmick was a success for the store. Dr. Thomas ended up buying a copy of the Rough Rider book for Lowell.

Arrangements were made with George Kyner. Lowell became a newsboy. The **Record** had been established 16 March 1895. While it was in print, the office was located at 118 South Fourth Street. The paper always had a healthy circulation, which was difficult since the district had some one hundred different papers published throughout its history. Lowell joined the newsboys' union just in time for the Labor Day Celebration.

Four thousand people from thirty-eight different unions composed the line of the parade on Victor Avenue. Twenty thousand congregated on the walkways to see the procession. Flags waved as the mile and a half parade marched. Twenty minutes passed before the parade completely went by any single place. The Victor Miners' Union was honored with the blue ribbon for the most attractive display.

Fifteen thousand people participated in the festivities that followed at Pinnacle Park. All thirty-five members of the Newsboys' union attended. They had their own foot race with a five-dollar first prize. Lowell did not take part in this particular contest. But he realized taking advantage of such opportunities in the future could easily raise the fifteen dollars he needed to buy his burro.

As soon as Lowell went to work at the **Record**, a tin can with the word "burro" painted on it was put up on a shelf for him in his home. The can held his savings. Unfortunately, he discovered that it would take more than fifteen dollars to purchase his burro. His father told him that he had to have more money so he could feed and shelter the animal. The news hardly discouraged him. It made him work with more enterprise.

The **Record** was a morning paper issued every day except Monday. At 3 A.M., Lowell rose from bed and prepared himself for work. He walked from his house on South Sixth Street to the **Record** office on South Fourth. When the papers were off the presses, he folded them in the back room of the **Record** building. Daylight slipping into the sky found Lowell already on his route.

The major part of his circuit was Victor's business section. This encompassed most of Third, Fourth, Fifth, and Sixth streets between Portland and Diamond avenues. The tenderloin on North First was another part of his route. He also delivered the **Record** in Goldfield.

At dawn, few people were on the streets. Occasionally, there were a couple of gamblers and drunks leaving a sporting house. Sometimes, in the tenderloin, a scantily dressed lady would come to the door as Lowell delivered the paper. She would be relieved to find only the newsboy. He would be asked in for a glass of milk. He would kindly refuse. His route was so extensive he had only a brief amount of time to dash off to school when he was finished.

Lowell always showed respect for the women in the tenderloin, even when he understood what they did for a living. When he bought his burro, he completed his route with time to spare. Then he would talk to the women. Many had interesting stories to tell. He saw that they were not mindless denizens of sin. Their words were compassionate, and their stories were filled with human drama.

To increase his income, he delivered **The Denver Post** to saloons and gaming houses. He became familiar with a type of life rarely spoken of in the Thomas residence. The only times the tenderloin was ever mentioned was when Dr. Thomas was city physician in 1906. Then, Dr. Thomas would come home with pitiful tales of ill-fortune and disease. As for Lowell, the ladies of North First Street were kind figures in the loneliness of the early morning hours in the City of Mines.

There was little debate amongst the people of Victor. The new opera house was a blessing. It brought culture to the town. Stephen G. Cunningham, as manager, was determined to please as many people as he could with his program schedule. In September, Cunningham brought in the dramatized version of Hall Caine's book, **The Penitent.** Hall Caine (Sir Thomas Henry) was an English novelist with whom Dr. Thomas was familiar. The alluring play contained comedy and pathos. The drama was performed by a company of actors from Boston, and was billed as a "flawless production".* Tickets were sold at Smith's Pharmacy, 108 North Third. All 1,200 seats were quickly bought.

The arts followed wealth, and there were constantly new riches being discovered in the district. A special guard was stationed at the Wild Horse Mine above Midway. Ore had been uncovered which assayed at ninety-nine ounces per ton--approximately $1,980 for every two thousand pounds of rock mined. The first eight hour shift brought out $12,000 worth of gold ore. The rock was said to be so rich that after handling it, a single rubbing on the trousers made them glisten in the sun.

14 September 1902, 9:35 Sunday night: Winfield Scott Stratton died in his Colorado Springs home, 115 North Weber Street. He had been unconscious since noon. He passed away peacefully. Although he was an eccentric man, he was one of the few millionaires of the Cripple Creek-Victor Mining District who returned to the area some of what he had taken out. His secretive life had spawned many rumors. He was said to have a special suite in Cripple Creek's National Hotel that had mirrors on the ceiling and all four walls. Curtailing his liaison with Pearl de Vere--Madame of the Old Homestead Parlour House, was purported to be the cause of her suicide. Raucous gambling parties were supposed to be held in his house near the Independence Mine. These rumors and others like them were temporarily quelled by eulogies.

Stratton was the man who had purchased entire blocks in Colorado Springs, then donated them to the city. He was the man who had saved Denver's Brown Palace Hotel from destruction by paying off its mortgage. He had given Colorado Springs it electric tramway system and Mining Exchange Building. Now he was dead. His attorney, Henry McAllister, Jr., announced that the majority of Stratton's twelve-million-dollar estate was to be used to establish the Myron Stratton Memorial Home in Colorado Springs for the orphaned and aged.

At the time of his death, more than $50,000 a month was being spent by his Cripple Creek Mining and Development Company to pursue his "Bowl of Gold" theory. His Lady Stith claim had reached the 1,300 foot level. The American Eagle mines were 1,750 feet deep. Orpha May Mine was some 1,200 feet down. And the Zenobia Mine was extended nearly 1,400 feet below the surface. Stratton had owned almost one-fifth of the district's richest properties.

His body was placed on display in the Mining Exchange Building in Colorado Springs on 17 September. Ten thousand people lined up on Nevada Avenue to view his body. The coffin was made of cedarwood. Its inner surface was copper-lined. The bevel-glass top stretched the full length of the coffin. A silver nameplate simply read: "1848--Winfield Scott Stratton--1902."

The Masons of the El Paso Chapter, Lodge No. 13 A.F. and A.M., performed the last rites at Evergreen Cemetery, 19 September. Roses and carnations made up the wreath. The ceremony was private.

McAllister informed named relatives they were to receive $50,000 each from Stratton's estate. Stratton's estranged son, I. Harry Stratton, was specifically warned not to contest the will. He ignored the warning and filed suit on 25 September.

The **Record** reported the district's gold production for 1902 to be $24,508,311 in approximately 1,225,415 troy ounces.

Stratton's Independence Mine sat at the bottom of Battle Mountain in the corner of Victor. It was the "bank" of one of the most interesting characters associated with the City of Mines. His beneficient deeds were only equaled by his eccentricities. When Stratton died, the town of Victor was forced into a new era--that of the corporation. Cripple Creek District Museum

The Baltimore Hotel, circa 1903. The fifty room hotel had been built before the Thomases arrived in Victor in 1900. Lowell Thomas' high school fraternity rented a room for their meetings in this building. The hotel sported two dining rooms and the German Beer Hall. When Lowell Thomas left Victor in 1912, the Baltimore was still a proud hotel. In later years, the hotel was demoslished.

Colorado Historical Society

Victor's Third Street, looking south. Armory Hall, immediate left, was a meeting place and dance hall. During the labor strike of 1903-04, this building was used as a prison.

Pioneer Museum

1903

The new year opened in tears for the Thomases. "Helen Wagoner (Wagner), baby daughter of Dr. and Mrs. H.G. Thomas, died yesterday (1 January) morning and will be buried from the family residence at 207 South Sixth Street this afternoon at 2 o'clock. The arrangements are in charge of the Dunn Undertaking Company and Rev. Forester (Forrester) will preach the sermon. Little Helen was only one year old and was the joy of the home which is now desolated by her death." The **Record** gave this report in its 2 January 1903 issue. The burial was performed at Sunnyside Cemetery. The Reverend R.H. Forrester, pastor of the Methodist Episcopal Church, spoke at the service while special music was played.

The **Record** printed the following eulogy for Helen Thomas on 5 January. "Helen Wagoner (Wagner) Thomas. The death angel sometimes comes unannounced and takes our dearest treasure. The home of Dr. and Mrs. H.G. Thomas was visited early Thursday morning and Helen, their infant daughter, was suddenly called home to be with God. Helen was born in Victor, December 13, 1901 and lingered to cheer and brighten her home for only a year and three weeks. She was certainly an angel messenger and, though the home is saddened, they are thankful for her short sweet visit. Helen was not only the pride of her home, but was admired and loved by all who knew her. She was an especially bright looking child and her face, so peaceful, told of the pure spirit within her. Is it any wonder she was called to live with the angels?

> 'Shall I have naught that is fair,
>   said he;
> Have naught but the hardened grain?
> Though the breath of these flowers is
>   sweet to me,
> I will give them all back again.'

"The funeral was largely attended and was conducted from the house at 2 P.M. Friday...The many friends of the sorrow-stricken family extend their deepest sympathy."

Seventy-nine years later, as Lowell Thomas was being driven past Sunnyside Cemetery, sorrow edged into his thoughts. Speaking in reference to his departed sister Helen, he said in an unfamiliar tone, "It's very sad. She never had a chance at life...she missed so very much."

In 1900, George E. Kyner was the secretary and general manager of the Victor **Daily Times**, Fourth Street and Diamond Avenue. He and his wife lived in an apartment in the **Times** building. Mrs. Kyner was a religious woman who attended services at the Methodist Episcopal Church. She was associated with Mrs. Thomas through the Epworth League, the Woman's Club, and the church choir. It had been recognized that Mrs. Kyner possessed an excellent singing voice. She was regularly called upon to sing solos in church and club functions. Through Mrs. Kyner's relation with Mrs. Thomas, one of Dr. Latimer's daughters, Valley, was given the opportunity to develop her singing talents.

George Kyner took over the Victor **Daily Record** as president of the Record Printing and Publishing Company. A subscription to the paper cost six dollars a year or sixty cents a month. Kyner boosted the **Record's** circulation to the largest in the district within one year of his acquisition of the newspaper. In April 1903, the Kyner's moved from the **Times** Building to a house at 325 South Fourth Street.

The Kyners were close friends of the Thomases, which would explain the unusually emotional eulogy printed for Helen Thomas in the **Record**. Eulogies of this kind were not commonly printed except for well-known people. Lowell was working for Kyner. Kyner liked Lowell's energetic spirit. The Thomas' friendship with the Kyners proved helpful in launching Lowell's newspaper career.

Delivering the paper early in the morning, spending the majority of the day in the classroom, and then rushing off to practice some sport did not leave time for much rest. The early hours and cold mornings gave the Thomases some worries. Lowell braved the circumstances, and that was enough to convince his parents that he could take care of himself. He was given something to think about, however, when Raymond Stein, a carrier for **The Denver Post,** was stopped by a gang of boys near Altman.

The gang surrounded Raymond's mount. They warned him not to deliver a *scab* paper. Altman was the highest point in the district. It was governed by the Western Federation of Miners (WFM) Union Local No. 19. The town had seceded from the United States during the labor war of 1894. In 1903, Altman was still predominantly pro-union. Any sort of anti-union activity, whether it be in the district or somewhere else in the state, caused the people of Altman to surge into an uproar.

The Denver Post was labeled a *scab*--anti-union--newspaper because it had favored the mine owners' position in a recent strike in Telluride, Colorado. The gang of boys did not force any violence upon Stein, but they were serious about preventing him from delivering the **Post** in Altman. Stein felt it wise to turn away from the confrontation.

Guards escorted Stein on his delivery route the following day. The fathers of the boys claimed the actions of their sons were not union-encouraged.

Lowell could not help but wonder if a similar incident would befall him on his Denver **Post** route through the saloons. Victor was also a center for the WFM. Altman had always been quick to react to any union situation. Victor was not as hasty. Lowell continued to deliver his papers.

In January 1903, Colorado was proclaimed the greatest precious metal producer in the country by the United States Director. Of the $27,502,429 in gold mined from the state in 1902, the Cripple Creek-Victor Mining

District was credited with supplying at least $17,000,000. The area around Victor produced more than eighty percent of that figure. Victor was the largest gold producer in all of America.

Drs. Thomas and Latimer had formed a partnership. Their offices were in rooms 4, 5, and 6 of the Boston Building on the northwest corner of Fourth and Victor Avenue. The office phone number was Victor 654-A. Other physicians and surgeons moved into the same location. The Boston Building was renamed the Physicians' Building.

Other aspects of the city were in the process of changing. The city council was again debating the closure of the Red Light Dance Hall. A vote was taken. Nothing could be decided.

A new electric suburban tram called the High Line was activated. On its route, it passed through Goldfield and Independence, around Battle Mountain, Bull Hill, Gold Hill, and Tenderfoot Hill. Its two end points were Victor and Cripple Creek. Now the district had two interurban tramway systems: the Low Line and the High Line.

News of a strike in the ore mills of Colorado City put Victor on the alert. WFM president, Charles Moyer, threatened to pull his union members out of the Cripple Creek-Victor mines if positive negotiations were not made in the mill workers' strike. Victor hoped the strike could be avoided. Most of the miners were not in favor of Moyer's threat. They were working for the highest wages in the region and did not care to upset that standing.

Word was made public 25 February that negotiations had been broke off between the strikers and the mill owners. Those immediately affected were the Telluride Company, the Portland Mill, and the Colorado City mills. The matter had turned sour. The strike became general 1 March. Starting at the Standard Plant of the United States Reduction and Refining Company, the strike spread through Colorado City, Telluride, and Leadville. Mine managers in the Cripple Creek-Victor Mining District continued shipping ore to Colorado City, but little of it was processed.

The Colorado National Guard was called in to protect the ore. Gatling guns were set up to prevent the strikers from attacking the mills. The Western Federation of Miners had all the encouragement they needed to start another war.

People in Victor occupied themselves with anything to avoid the thought of another labor confrontation.

H.H. Bourk and Company, 116 South Fourth Street, advertised Edison phonographs for thirty-five dollars apiece. New molded records were a quarter. The McGee Mercantile Company suggested five different grades of Waldorf Astoria coffee and two grades of Ben Hur coffee as superb morning stimulants. They also promoted California apricots at twelve-and-a-half cents a can, a gallon can of pumpkin for thirty cents, and Crackerjack Corn for ten cents. Shilling's Clothing Store had a new line of women's apparel: walking shirts for four dollars, kimonos with embroidery and applique starting at sixty-five cents, percale wrappers, and one hundred and fifty new dresses.

18 March: Charles Moyer called out eight hundred and twenty-five men from the Cripple Creek-Victor mines. Stratton's Independence lost four hundred and fifty miners. The Granite Mine lost seventy-five men, and the Ajax one hundred and twenty-five. Nonunion miners began replacing the strikers 25 March. Their arrival coincided with the closing of the Vindicator Mine. Matters worsened when Charlie MacNeill's Canon City mill was destroyed by fire. Arson was suspected.

1 April headlines of the **Record** spelled out, "STRIKE POSITIVELY SETTLED." The words were not convincing.

Senator Wolcott joined I. Henry Stratton's suit contesting W.S. Stratton's will. Wolcott was out to prove that the elder Stratton had been immoral and insane when the will had been drawn up. Wolcott's haughty brashness in Victor in 1900 had already been forgotten. The case was decided on 7 April. I.H. Stratton was granted $350,000 instead of $50,000. After lawyers' fees and court costs, he was left with $172,000.

W.E. Dingman, A. Wright, H. Wright, S. Bascom, and C.L. Lamb were arrested in Victor on charges of gambling. The Law and Order League was cleaning up the district again. Dingman and his *gang* were incarcerated for openly conducting poker games in a cigar store. The League struck one more axe in the bar for the salvation of humanity.

The literary set of Victor was treated to superb plays at the Victor Opera House. Florence Roberts appeared in Alphonse Daudet's **Sapho** on Sunday, 12 April. This was followed by a special production of William Shakespeare's **The Merchant of Venice** on Tuesday, 12 May. Charles B. Hanford and Miss Marie Drofnah, along with a company of twenty players, staged this elaborate show. Mary Shaw came to town on 18 May in Henrick Isben's **Ghosts.** These were definitely splendid theatrical offerings which Dr. and Mrs. Thomas would not have missed.

Samuel Underwood, Ben Goldworthy, and Will Goldworthy were working the Wilson claim near Altman. They were two hundred feet underground and seventy-five feet into the drift. It was near the end of their shift and the last of eight giant powder charges was being tamped by Underwood. The charge exploded. Underwood's head was almost torn from his body. His face was obliterated. He died instantly. The Goldworthy brothers suffered severe lacerations.

Underwood was twenty-eight years old, married four years, and had one child. He had been a popular member of Altman's Miners' Union No. 19. His body was taken to Dunn Undertaking in Victor.

Victor's Washington School children went on strike 20 May. It started when Clarence Urquhart's sister had her mouth washed out with quinine and salts by her fourth grade teacher. She had been chewing gum in class. When news of the incident circulated among the children, they decided to walk out.

Outside the school, teachers struggled to get the children to return to classes. The children retaliated by throwing stones and other missiles. Truant Officer Reedy was called to the scene. The striking students were rounded up and hauled off to Judge Frost's court for punishment.

Fire broke out in the Altman Hotel on Baldwin Avenue at 2 P.M. on 22 May. The fire department quickly responded, but their water supply had been cut off. Soon, Altman's entire business section was in flames. Other fire departments from the rest of the district rumbled in to the rescue. They, too, were thwarted by the lack of water.

Buildings had to be blown up to stop the fire from consuming the whole town. Within hours, losses exceeded $40,000. Suspicions of arson were confirmed. Charges were filed against John Lyons and Mrs. Ollie Davisson.

Tensions prevailed between union and nonunion men. Especially after C.C. Hamlin, Secretary of the Mine Owners Association, announced that the organization intended to purge the Cripple Creek-Victor Mining District of all the Western Federation of Miners' influence. Violence became common.

T.M. Stewart, who lived near the Midland Terminal Depot in Victor, was assaulted by five men. After being fiercely beaten, he was shot in the back, point-blank. A few days later, the home of John Dennison caught fire. The house was on the south slope of Beacon Hill, close to the El Paso Mine. Arson was confirmed. The Citizens Alliance was formed to help combat the increasing incidents of violence.

But the Alliance only helped to cause further strife in the district. Governor Peabody sent a committee up to Victor to discuss the problems. The committee held a closed meeting with the mine owners. The Citizens' Alliance wanted the Colorado National Guard to mediate the situation.

The miners' union issued a warning in the **Record:** "No Troops Are Needed Here." The warning was not heard. 4 September: the National Guard arrived in the area. Sherman Bell, a member of Victor's Knights of Pythias and once one of Roosevelt's Rough Riders, was given command of the militia. Camp French was formed at a suitable point just beyond the Independence Mine.

A group of men tried blowing up Sam Tack's house in the town of Independence. The stick of dynamite was poorly thrown and only a small portion of the home was damaged. Tack's home near the Dante Mine was made an example of the union's defiance of the mine owners. Listings of fights, shootings, and dynamitings became a regular column in the **Record.**

The unrest in the district limited some but not all of Lowell's and Jay's activities. Lowell was eleven and in the seventh grade. Smoking was popular with the boys. Watching the men outside the saloons and parlour houses roll up their own cigarettes encouraged the boys to take up the "sport". They would hike to the mouth of the United Mines Transportation Tunnel in Eclipse Gulch. Among the dormant buildings of the Woods' Economic Extraction Mill, Lowell and Jay practiced rolling their Bull Durham or Duke's Mixture. The tobacco was the courtesy of W.E. Dingman.

Lowell's parents neither smoked nor drank. Dr. and Mrs. Thomas preferred spending their money on books. Lowell respected his parents views. He smoked to be "one of the boys". Upon his arrival in Victor, he had wanted to be accepted by the other children. They had called him "Rube" when they learned he had come from Iowa. Then, he was called "Windy" when they found out his father was giving him oratory lessons. Lowell was determined to fit in with the rest, even if it meant ignoring some of the rules his parents had laid down for him. He could not be a leader unless he had a group to lead.

After Lowell and Jay accomplished rolling their own cigarettes, they discovered Henry IV cigars. The nausea they caused unequaled anything Lowell would ever smoke. Except charas. In 1921, Lowell was waiting to enter into the "Forbidden Land" of Afghanistan. While in Peshawar, he was introduced to a mixture of hemp, camel dung, and tobacco called charas. He did not try to accustom himself to the Afghani pastime.

His cigarette habit persisted until he became editor of the Victor **Daily Record** in 1911. As editor, he was responsible for the entire paper. There was little time to smoke. Lowell dropped his eight year habit and never returned to it.

7 September 1903: Lowell marched in the Labor Day parade. Because of the unrest in Victor, Altman, and Goldfield, the parade was held in Cripple Creek. Four thousand people joined the march. It took one hour to completely go by any one particular store on Bennett Avenue. The forty members of the Victor Newsboys' Union No. 32 were all dressed in white duck suits. Union No. 32 won first honors. Lowell was part of the newboys' union.

As a prize, the union was given five dollars for their treasury. Each boy was awarded free run of Pinnacle Park for the remainder of the day. The festivities were sponsored by Altman's Miners' Union No. 19.

The Labor Day Celebration was the last major gathering to take place in the district for many months. After meeting with A.E. Carlton and other members of the mine owners' committee, General Sherman Bell declared all large congregations in the district to be unlawful. Bell then proceeded to build a "bull pen" in Goldfield for military prisoners. Within hours, men were taken from their homes and tossed into the pen. Men designated for the "bull pen" by militia were supposed to be union trouble makers.

Patrick J. Lynch, a county commissioner, was arrested in his home. Lynch was a peaceable citizen. He was arrested at his dinner table. Without legal papers, he was locked in the "bull pen." Judge Reilly of Independence was also arrested and put in the pen. Reilly was accused of inciting men to boycott their jobs.

17 September was the day the entire district was converted into a prison camp. General Bell set up heliograph stations and enormous searchlights on Bull Hill, Nipple Mountain, Gold Hill, and Raven Hill. Telegraph stations were established on Bull, Mineral, and Beacon hills. He placed field telephones in every camp and on Tenderfoot Hill, Battle Mountain, and Cow Mountain. Bell was preparing to fight a war.

Solar lamps were placed on Cow, Pisgah, and Straub mountains, and also on St. Peter's Dome. Twelve powerful telescopes were mounted at strategic locations. To guard these preparations, Bell had gatling guns and cannons at his command. He also issued a decree: anyone attempting to destroy or disrupt the militia's designated stations would face a $100 to $1,000 fine, and up to three years in jail. Bell did not realize he had already turned the whole district into one huge penitentiary. The people of the area were bound to act like rebellious prisoners.

Putting on a show of force, a company of soldiers surrounded Stratton's Independence Mine. One of Bell's menacing gatling guns was placed on a tall ore dump overlooking Victor. The men working in the mine were dismissed, and the ever-important water pumps were shut off. Bell was looking for a fight. But so were Charles Moyer and Bill Haywood of the Western Federation of Miners.

Moyer wanted the WFM to be a key force in the state of Colorado. Haywood was Moyer's wrath-wielding tool. When it appeared the miners would no longer support the Colorado City mill workers' strike, Haywood had Harry Orchard and Steve Adams blow up something.

The district was primed for one of the worst labor wars in its history.

Amidst building anxieties, the people of Victor pushed on with their daily lives. The Woman's Club inaugurated a literature and art department. Their first meeting was at 2:30 in the afternoon of 19 September in the Masonic Hall, 114-116 South Fourth Street. "The Round Table" was the special feature. Literary papers were read and discussed. Mrs. Thomas had the honor of presenting the group's first paper. Her subject was "Toltecs and Aztecs."

The rest of the town went on with its business. The Union Meat Market, 410 West Victor Avenue, had coffee for sale at reduced prices. Ben Hur brands were thirty-five cents per tin. Santos Coffee, either Mocha or Java, was twelve and a half cents a pound. Faust and Old Indian coffees were forty-five cents a cannister. In competition, the Simonton-Moore Mercantile Company, 110 North Fourth, offered Richelieu Coffee at a special price of forty cents a tin. Creamery butter was twenty-five cents a pound. Pride of the Rockies Flour was two dollars and twenty-five cents per hundred pounds at Gagen's Grocery, 122 South Fourth.

The cost of groceries did not concern "Czar Bell", as the **Record** called him. If he needed foodstuffs for his troops, he had them confiscated from the nearest union store. Edible supplies were constantly dwindling in Bell's camps, due mostly to the large amount of men imprisoned in the "bull pens". Their number grew at an alarming rate.

Judge Seeds, of the county courthouse in Cripple Creek, issued writs of "habeas corpus" for four prominent men alleged to be in the Goldfield pen. Seeds wanted them in his court by 21 September. Bell complied with the legal action. However, before these men were seen, two companies of cavalry took possession of the courthouse. Guards were stationed at every entrance. Twenty men with rifles poured into the building. Another hundred troops surrounded the outer grounds. A gatling gun was set up in the street, and special marksmen were placed atop the buildings at the intersection of Fourth and Bennett Avenue.

The district was shocked by Bell's military display. The breaking point was near. That night, sentries around Strong's Camp shot at something moving in the dark. Bullets went flying through two houses. Searchlights located the intruder. The sentries had killed a grazing burro.

22 September: Bell informed Judge Seeds that three of the four men who had appeared in court would be released to civil authorities. When Bell's decision was rescinded, the miners talked of storming the "bull pen". To ward off threats, Bell sent one hundred cavalrymen to break into the Victor Ball Park on East Victor Avenue and ready a cannon for firing.

Drs. Thomas and Cohen performed emergency surgery on Arthur Kavanaugh. The boy's left lung had formed a lethal abcess. His life depended on its removal. Arthur was the son of E.J. Kavanaugh, owner of Kavanaugh and Babcock Cigars and Tobacco, 217 South First Street. Arthur was the librarian of the Gold Coin Club.

Part of Arthur's sixth rib was removed in the operation. The doctors' work was successful. But the boy's condition was weak. Complications caused the boy's death a week after the operation.

Bell's military prowess was made into something of a farce when a raid was staged on Altman's Miners' Union No. 19, 25 September. Two hundred troops were engaged in the action. The Union Hall on East Main Street was surrounded at nine in the evening. The troops forced their way in. The lights were on, but no one was inside.

The soldiers were directed to capture the three saloons in Altman. The Apex and Monte Carlo saloons, both on Baldwin Avenue, were stormed and seized. Again, no miner was found. Nor could the soldiers find Altman's third saloon. Nearly eleven thousand feet above sea level, Altman had only nine hundred residents and one main street. Still, the soldiers could not locate the third saloon.

Most of the members of Local Number 19 were drinking in the Grand View Saloon. The Grand View was in Midway. The soldiers were not aware that the small village of Midway, at the foot of Bull Hill, was considered part of Altman. After maneuvering up and down Altman proper, the soldiers became bored.

The two hundred troops headed towards Elkton. They arrested Marshal Joe Lynch of Independence along the way. Marching into Elkton, they broke into the Yeoman's meeting place. Finding nothing else devoid of miners to raid, they played piano and milked cows for amusement.

26 September: Striker's Clothing Store, 118 North Third Street, opened a full page ad in the **Record** with, "Keep Out of the Bull Pen and don't think out loud while the militia tarries here. You can think, privately, however, without being arrested...." The ad went on to list the "good buys" at the store. "Children's Union Suits in gray, very good quality, at 25¢. Flannelette Wrappers, all sizes, $1.00...."

The inevitable raid on the union's "mouthpiece", the Victor **Daily Record**, occurred on 29 September 1903. At 10:55 P.M., during the most hectic hour for a morning paper, the militia forced their way into the **Record** building under the command of Major Tom E. McClelland. The linotypes were already in action and the foreman was "rushing" the proofs. Two companies of infantry, two troops of cavalry, and a gatling gun were deployed to arrest five newspapermen.

After a vile discourse and a blatant denial of rights, George E. Kyner, managing editor, H.J. Richmond, foreman, F.W. Langdon, linotype operator, Charles G. Langdon, linotype operator, and W.L. Sweet, circulator, were taken prisoner and hauled off to Camp Goldfield. "It was a deliberate plot to suppress a paper for telling the truth about the uniformed hirelings who were guilty of the outrages...."[10] Emma Langdon, wife of Charles G. Langdon, was awakened by Mrs. Kyner. The paper was to be printed despite the militia's actions.

Mrs. Langdon ran the linotype. A.Q. Miller, business manager of the **Record**, completed the proofs. Mr. Conrad acted as pressman. At 3 A.M., just as the newsboys arrived, the paper was ready. Lowell was amongst the boys who braved the troops to deliver the paper.

The large headline of the paper, "SOMEWHAT DISFIGURED, BUT STILL IN THE RING!" told the story. A centered and boxed article just below read, "The Record Office was raided by the military last night shortly before eleven o'clock and all that was mortal of the office force was forthwith marched to a place on Battle Mountain called the 'bull pen'." Mrs. Langdon visited the "pen" herself at 6 A.M. to deliver the morning edition to Mr. Kyner.

Attorney Tully Scott arranged for the newspapermen to be set free on bond. J.H. Williams, W.J. Donnelly, E.M. Ovren, and J. Murphy raised the necessary $13,000. The five men were turned over to Sheriff Robertson of Teller County, and then informed that they had been arrested as defendents in a libel case. The Victor Typographical Union No. 275 entered a formal protest in the district's court against the militia's actions.

Emma Langdon wrote a book about the 1903-04 labor war called **The Cripple Creek Strike**. The Victor **Daily Record** published the first edition in 1904. In her book, Mrs. Langdon claimed, "The real reason of the military raiding the office at that hour, was to suppress the official organ of the Western Federation of Miners."[11] If this was so, the Colorado

National Guard did not accomplish what it had set out to do. If anything, the paper's circulation increased.

Not everyone in Victor was oppressed by the militia's presence. Some found ways to profit from their stay. After the **Record** reported that many of the troops were experiencing severe colds due to inadequate shelter and long duty hours, the Central Drug Company came up with an ingenious idea. Taking out a large ad on page two of the **Record,** the company's new drug, "Mountain Sage" was recommended as a specific for curing colds. This miraculous medicine was manufactured exclusively by the Central Drug Company. It also purported the relief of "hay fever, chill, torpid liver, headache and neuralgia." Supposedly, it contained no addictive drugs, but it was a stimulant and diuretic. The Central Drug Company, southeast corner of Fourth and Victor Avenue, had a difficult time keeping up with the demand for their new medicine.

Another major *disease* plaguing Bell's soldiers was boredom. The cure for this ailment was liquor. Hayner Whiskey, pure seven-year-old rye, sold for a dollar a quart. Roy Campbell of the Meeker Cavalry already had too much whiskey in him when he burst into the Kentucky Club Saloon in Victor. He immediately started shouting and chasing patrons out of the saloon. He ordered the bartender to close the establishment. When the bartender refused, Campbell went for his gun. Before it left his holster, Officer Jack Burnham had a .38 calibre Colt at Campbell's throat. Burnham escorted the private to the city jail. The Meeker Cavalry rode into Victor to demand Campbell's release. Burnham refused until the prisoner was sober. The Meeker Cavalry rode out of town.

4 November: the doors of the Woods' First National Bank of Victor was closed. This action was performed under the direction of the currency comptroller. The bank's examiner declared the institution insolvent. This had resulted from "losses sustained by reason of excessive accommodations extended to certain mining interests with which the officers of the bank were connected."* The Woods' had built the foundations of their financial empire on faltering investments. Frank M. Woods stated that the closure of the bank was due to low cash reserves in comparison with outstanding loans and discounts. He promised every depositor would be paid in full. The bank's doors remained permanently closed.

D.H. Moffat kept his Bank of Victor open until 4:30 P.M. to accommodate customers effected by the First National's closure. A.E. Carlton, president of the First National Bank of Cripple Creek, made a statement "To depositors of the First National Bank of Victor...we will loan 25 percent of such deposit at 8% per year...To avoid embarrassment to our local people during the present financial disturbance...."* Financial competitors swooped down upon the Woods' dying establishment.

The Woods' empire had already been overextended. The strike helped to push them over the brink. With few miners working, production was low. The Woods' thin cash flow quickly ran dry. After all the Woods had done for the miners, the strike of 1903-04 signaled the end of their reign in Victor.

The energy of the strike had reached a low point. Through veiled means, word passed from Bill Haywood to Harry Orchard that something must be done to revive the power of the strike. Orchard went to work with what he knew best--dynamite.

Eleven seconds after eleven in the morning, over fifty pounds of dynamite exploded on the six-hundred-foot level of the Vindicator Mine. Harry Orchard and Billy Aikman thought they had set the trap on the seven-hundred-foot level where a group of nonunion miners had been working. Instead, Orchard had confused the levels and set the explosive device in a dormant drift. Two well-liked union men, Superintendent Charles McCormick and Melvin Beck, were blown apart. Timbers eighteen inches square were cut off in the middle by the blast. Ventilation pipes were broken and bent. Both McCormick and Beck were lying in pieces at the bottom of a huge hole which the dynamite had ripped out of the floor.

Only a few remnants of a 32-calibre revolver and the wire which tied the explosive device to the cage were found. Size eight shoeprints were discovered, but no definite leads could be found. The Mine Owners Association offered $5,000 for information leading to the arrest and conviction of the perpetrators of the crime. Neither Orchard nor Aikman were linked to the murders. General Bell increased his arrest quota.

Haywood and Moyer were pleased with Orchard's actions. The strike was ready to turn into war again. Orchard was sent three hundred dollars and told to be prepared for similar jobs.

The district went beserk with violence. Senseless arrests were rampant. Miners armed themselves and roved the hillsides looking for trouble. More guards patroled the towns. People lost control of their anxieties.

Mrs. George Fuller entered the Atlantic Tea Company, 204 East Bennett Avenue, and for no apparent reason started disrobing. The management rushed to the scene and pleaded with her to leave the store. By the time she reached her undergarments, she was ready to move on. She ran down the street to 212 East Bennett and flew into the Bazaar Dry Goods Store. Frenzied, she tore at the rest of her clothes until she was in "her neat union suit".* Four policemen tried subduing her. She fought them off viciously, laughing all the while in a demonic voice.

Finally, they cornered her. Mrs. Fuller was arrested. Naked, she was carted off to the police station. She recovered her reason late that night at headquarters. She could give no explanation for her temporary insanity.

Going to the Frisco Liquor House, 105 South Third Street, and buying a couple of quarts of "Union Label Whiskey" seemed the only sane thing to do.

The gold production for the year slipped to $17,630,107, according to the Victor **Daily Record.**

Victor celebrates. A southerly view of the intersection of Fourth Street and Victor Avenue, 1905. The town has rejuvenated after the Strike of 1903-04. To the right, the vacant lot which had been the site of the 6 June 1904 riot has been converted into a showcase for entertainment. The Boston Clothing Store can be plainly seen. Lowell Thomas had watched the 1904 riot from the window second from the left.

Colorado Historical Society

This riot on 6 June 1904 ended the reign of the Western Federation of Miners in the district forever. A vacant lot on the corner of Fourth and Victor Avenue had often served as an area for patriotic celebrations. On 6 June 1904, this lot was used by C.C. Hamlin, the Mine Owners Association, and the Colorado National Guard to destroy the WFM. Dr. Thomas' medical office was on the southwest corner of this intersection at the time.

Cripple Creek District Museum

1904

The year crept in on a bare and quivering aspen branch. News from the district was bleak. Everyone pointed fingers at everyone else, not knowing who would snap the winter-gnarled branch first.

Business went on. At H.H. Rosser's store, 112 North Fourth Street, all sorts of smoking pipes were for sale: meerschaum and briar, gold and silver, mounted or plain. Rosser stocked a fine assortment of tobacco and cigars. Twenty-five cents bought the latest from the Columbia Phonograph Company. Mr. H.H. Rosser also operated a poolroom.

Rosser had a large build and a red moustache. His hall had six pool tables and many slot machines. Lowell became familiar with the pool hall while on his paper route. He learned how to play billiards in Rosser's store. The slot machines were another temptation. Lowell's conscious weighed heavy. "Nor could I take any comfort from the fact that my parents, who often inveighed against gambling at cards, had never mentioned slot machines."[12] He continued to lose nickels in Rosser's store.

Modern vaudeville was popular at the Crystal Theater, 109 South Third Street. Admission was ten cents. Matinees cost children a nickel. Lowell and Jay liked the theater, including vaudeville. J. Turner Wall, a Hawaiian comedian, played the Crystal 30 April. Wall's claim to fame was the manner in which he sang, "Tain't No Disgrace to Run When You Are Scared". Moving pictures such as **The Great Train Robbery** were shown. Live acts like Howard Morris as "The World's Greatest Rag Time Whistler", Downey and Willard in the comedy sketch "A Dutchman's Troubles", and many others would follow. Between vaudeville at the Crystal Theater and literary productions at the Victor Opera House, Lowell was exposed to the values of both entertainment and education.

Football became a part of Lowell's life when he was twelve. A level place to play the game was not easy to find. Rules were contoured to the shape of the field. Practice was strenuous. But it helped to keep him active.

As the football games grew in popularity, a wide range of children gathered at the field. Lowell remembered one large girl in particular known as "Red." She was constantly waiting on the sidelines to play. Most of the boys paid no attention to her. One day her chance came. A team was short a player and she was the only feasible substitute.

Once "Red" was in the game, she surprised everyone. She could pass, kick, tackle, receive, and run as well as any of the top players. No one questioned why "Red" played so keenly. She became one of the most sought after team members.

It was not until "Red's" voice changed and she grew whiskers on her face that Lowell and the other boys realized "Red" was male. "Red" was the sixth son of parents hoping for a daughter. To cover up their inability to have a female child, his parents dressed and treated him like a girl. After "Red's" secret was exposed, he never returned to the playing field.

Victor was full of such surprises. The town thrived on odd quirks of fate and nature. Lowell absorbed the atmosphere of the area into his character as if it were his life's blood. Men who pursued gold were adventurous. Wherever they were, adventure was sure to be the mother-lode. Lowell could not help becoming part of all he experienced.

The Labor War of 1903-04 effected him profoundly. Living through the turbulent events of the time ignited the trait of courage within him. Working as a newsboy, delivering papers in the lonely morning hours while the tensions of labor strife were all around, strengthened Lowell's stamina. Exposure to violence made him accustomed to the misfortunes of war.

The strike was in another stalemate. In June, many miners were back at work.

Word had come from the St. Louis World's Fair that Victor's own John E. Smith Pharmacy, 108 North Third Street, was winner of the first prize in the ice cream contest. It was relayed to the world that the best tasting ice cream anywhere was manufactured in Victor, Colorado. Victor had something to be proud of again no matter how trivial. Lowell, having cherished the taste of ice cream for some time, was already aware of the treats served in the Smith Pharmacy.

Charles Moyer and Bill Haywood were not impressed with the ice cream award. They were concerned that their strike was failing. They contacted Harry Orchard. Supplies were bought. One hundred pounds of dynamite and two boxes of detonators were taken by Orchard to the house of Steve Adams. Late into the night of 5 June, Orchard and Adams went to work.

At 2:15 A.M. on 6 June, an explosion rocked the district. The train depot near the town of Independence was blown apart. Thirteen men died.

The hundred pounds of dynamite had been placed under the depot two yards from the railroad track. A revolver had been positioned to fire directly into the nitroglycerin blasting caps. Fifty yards from the depot, the wire was pulled. More than two dozen nonunion miners were caught in the explosion.

Phil Chandler was one of the last men to reach the depot's platform as the train pulled up to the west end. He was stepping onto the platform when the explosion ripped through the building. The platform was suddenly blown into pieces. Windows were shattered. Foundation posts were uprooted. Timbers from the depot were shot hundreds of feet in all directions. Shards of wood and metal tore through the air.

Across the road, a heavy rod pierced the house of Tim Collins, breaking a large hole in the north wall and lodging itself in the floor. Flying debris wrecked glass and wood as it traveled through the house in a shotgun pattern.

The force of the explosion flung the bodies of the men over a hundred-foot radius. Before four A.M., searchlights and rescuers combed the area for the injured and dead.

The sight of the depot area was gruesome. Bits of flesh were caught on branches. Pieces of bodies were found atop buildings and mine dumps. Maimed men were scattered all about, moaning and screaming for help.

Dr. Thomas was called upon, as were most of the other doctors in Victor and Goldfield. Phil Chandler was one of the fortunate. He was treated at the Red Cross Hospital for a broken ankle. Many of the injured could only be saved through amputation. Edward Molland lost his right leg. John Pollice had both legs removed.

William S. Shanklin, George M. Kelso, James Hartsock, Arthur Muehlsein, Alex McLain, Gus Augustine, Adam Ross, Henry Haag, S.G. Henderson, W.W. DeLano, a man known only as Johnson, Herb McCoy, and Robert Sin Clair all died so Harry Orchard could win Bill Haywood's gratitude. The killing was not over.

Bodies taken to Dunn's Undertaking were removed and placed in Hunt's Undertaking Company when the coroner at Dunn's suggested the depot explosion was an accident. All of the anxieties of the past twelve months were ready to resurface. The Independence Depot explosion was no accident.

A general meeting was called by the Mine Owners Association. Over a thousand people gathered in the vacant lot on the northeast corner of Fourth and Victor Avenue. Men, women, and children--union and nonunion--congregated to hear what C.C. Hamlin had to say.

Dr. Thomas had returned to his office. Lowell and Carl were also in the Physicians' Building directly across the street from the large gathering. They had come to Dr. Thomas' office to assist him. They looked out the window of the office when Hamlin started to speak.

Hamlin stood in a wagon and railed vehemently against the union. He decried the dynamiting of the depot. He blamed all the current strife in the district on the union's obstinancy. The crowd was prepared for battle. They only needed Hamlin to push them a little further. When he yelled out that all union men should be deported from the district, the battle cry was heard.

A shot rang out. Hamlin fell from the wagon. Some thought he had been killed. Gunfire responded from all points. People scattered, running from flying lead. Hamlin picked himself up and darted off for cover.

Roxie McGee caught a bullet. Shot through the heart, McGee died instantly.

John Davis was beaten over the head with a revolver butt. Lying helpless on the ground, he was shot in the back. Davis died at the Victor Hospital.

Peter Chrisman felt a bullet enter his left cheek, then embed itself in his jaw. Dr. Cohen treated Chrisman in his office. Chrisman recovered.

Dr. Thomas, Lowell, and Carl witnessed the shooting of J.J. Hosner. The bullet entered Hosner's left shoulder and lodged itself in his abdomen. Dr. Thomas ran into the street after Hosner. An unidentified man helped him bring Hosner up to his office.

Lowell and Carl continued to watch the riot, hoping Carl's father was not in the crowd. His safety was their concern.

Fred A. Studebass was shot in the left side. The shot had come from the Miners' Union Hall on Fourth Street, just east of the vacant lot. Soldiers from Company L arrived on the scene. A rifleman emptied his weapon into the mass of fleeing people. J.P. Murphy suffered a bullet wound in the back. Attorney Sam D. Crump was injured as the crowd trampled him.

A group of men took refuge in the union hall. Many of them were union cardholders. Company L surrounded the building and demanded their surrender. When no word was sent from the men in the union hall, the soldiers fired into the building. Bullets showered the structure for nearly three-fourths of an hour. Finally, a white handkerchief was hung out a window on the second floor.

Sixty men were herded from the building. Cory Thomas was among them. As prisoners, they were taken to Armory Hall. Edward McKelvey had been shot in the buttocks. He was taken to Dr. Latimer. Peter Calderwood was wounded in his right leg. John Reed had been shot in the back. Thomas McManus received a flesh wound of the leg. Chris Miller and Peter Brown both suffered scalp wounds from beatings.

Still, the terror did not end. Before the day was through, over one hundred men were locked up in Armory Hall. Soldiers and civilians destroyed what was left of the union hall. Gangs roamed the district beating union men and vandalizing union stores.

Dr. Thomas operated on J.J. Hosner. Lowell aided him in some of the minor tasks. Hosner's condition was serious, but Dr. Thomas' skill as a surgeon stabilized his body functions.

Lowell had unbuckled Hosner's gunbelt and placed it behind a bookshelf. Hosner recovered, but he never paid his bill. When Lowell showed Hosner's property to his father, suggesting the gun could substitute for payment, Dr. Thomas frowned. He returned the gun and holster to Hosner. But the medical bill was left unpaid.

By 8 June, one hundred and fifty men had been placed under arrest. Governor Peabody and General Bell declared martial law throughout Teller County.

Twenty-five miners were deported on 8 June. They were taken to the Short Line Depot, transported to Colorado Springs, and warned never to come back to the Cripple Creek-Victor Mining District. Ultimately, two hundred and twenty-five men were deported. Their families followed them.

Cory Thomas decided to leave of his own volition. He considered moving to Tonapah, Nevada, or the Alaskan Klondike. They were gone before the end of the summer.

The district was permanently altered. For a decade, it had been a haven for the WFM and other unions. After the Independence Depot incident and the Victor riot, the entire district was metamorphosized into one enormous company town.

Martial law remained in effect until the end of June. The Portland was one of the first mines to reopen. It was totally nonunion property.

For nearly a year, the people of Victor had lived under the constant threat of a labor war. The effect of such tension developed into many things. For Lowell, courage had been instilled into his personality. The violent experiences of those twelve months prepared him for danger.

He had witnessed shootings, beatings, murders--all the ugliness of war. He did not accept these as common human interactions. But he was exposed to such inhumanities, and thus he was not shocked by violence in his later life. Being able to cope with the bloody ways of war allowed him to dive into the middle of combat and report objectively on what he saw. Behind the ugliness he knew he would find a human story. To find this story, a fine reporter would often have to brave the perils of life.

Lowell's perception of human strife and interactions had been sharpened. The tumultuous labor war prepared him for a career as a war correspondent. In World War I, his bravery led him to the French and Italian fronts. It helped him to seek out T.E. Lawrence's unique story in Arabia. His courage even led him into revolutionary Germany after all the borders had been sealed off.

January 1919: Berlin. The Sparticist revolution was about to reach a climax. No outsiders were supposed to be in Germany. But Lowell knew there was an important story to be covered, so he and a friend, Webb Waldron, found their way into the "forbidden country."

They reported the daily events to the Associated Press. One day, Lowell and Webb were moving cautiously down Unter den Linden when machinegun fire broke out. Lowell's hat was shot off. A German reporter sent out a story stating Lowell Thomas had been shot through the heart. A friend on **The Denver Post** picked up the cable and told Lowell's wife, Fran. For two weeks, Fran Thomas thought she was a widow.

Lowell and Webb continued reporting on the German revolution until decisive events spelled out the country's future. They were the only American reporters in Germany. Their stories were exclusives for all the

American papers. Throughout their stay, their lives were in constant danger. But they persisted, knowing the whole world was concerned about the human drama in revolutionary Germany.

What Lowell had experienced and learned in Victor came into play repeatedly throughout his later life. Victor was a large part of Lowell's personality. He would never forget it.

The strike of 1903-04 was not easily erased from the minds of the people who had lived through it. When the Fourth of July came around in 1904, many people traveled to Colorado Springs or Denver to celebrate. The lively, patriotic spirit of the previous years could not be conjured up in the district with the smell of dynamite and blood still in the air.

On 5 July, the Short Line was returning from Colorado Springs with an abundance of passengers. The train stopped at Cameron to recouple cars. The procedure went awry. A car with over one hundred passengers broke loose and rolled backwards down the tracks. The steep grade of the hill allowed the car to swiftly pick up speed.

The brakeman could not engage the mechanism. People jumped from the engineless car. Almost seventy passengers had escaped before it became unsafe to jump. About a mile from where the car broke free, a man risked a leap. He collided with a boulder, and his body rolled limply down the embankment.

Approximately one and a half miles from Cameron, the car derailed itself and crashed into the far bank of a deep ravine. A special train was already on its way to the accident. The **Record** reported, "Drs. Thomas and Driscoll were the first to reach the sides of the injured and worked inces(s)antly for those who needed immediate attention." Drs. Cohen and Latimer arrived shortly thereafter.

T.P. Airheart, Joseph P. Kearns, and Dr. H.F. Torrance were the only passengers killed. Forty-nine suffered varying degrees of injury.

Despite the desperate events of 1904, the area did not lose its magic for Lowell. It "may have been in a decline, but I didn't know it. It remained for me--and remains to this day--alive and tantalizing."[13]

The character of the town still possessed a mystique which attracted a wide array of interesting people. A Madam Henry advertised her services as a clairvoyant in late August. She lived in the Central Rooming House near the corner of Third and Victor Avenue. She was respected for her accurate tarot card readings. But her specialty was locating mines through her crystal ball.

Warrants were issued for Harry Orchard and J.J. Neville in connection with the Independence Depot incident. Orchard and Neville had escaped to Wyoming long before. Steve Adams had also disappeared.

The Reverend T.S. Leland, pastor of the Methodist Church, was under investigation for harboring fugitives from justice. Leland had joined the WFM in 1903, and was making two hundred and fifty dollars a month lecturing on behalf of the union. He was arrested in Pueblo while speaking to a large assembly.

Late in October, word was passed around that a mysterious stranger was selling a special concoction to saloons. Five drops of this wondrous potion was supposed to turn a glass of water into whiskey. Some of the disillusioned buyers were complaining. The **Record** took it upon itself to warn the stranger to leave town before "he is shot or sent to Kentucky to be hanged."

30 October: J.E. Bryan became the new pastor of the Methodist Church.

Lowell and Jay attended Sunday services at the church in Anaconda. Their actions puzzled their parents. The Methodist Church was much closer than the church in Anaconda. The boys shared an attraction for the organist of Anaconda's church. Marie Guinan was a pretty girl from Waco, Texas. The boys were captivated by Marie's outstanding features and charismatic personality. When Miss Guinan moved to New York and became Texas Guinan, the boys lost their interest in the Anaconda church.

In his eighth grade class, Lowell's conduct did not make the best impression. He constantly made his presence known through some prank, sarcastic remark, or other nonsense. His object was to gain attention, not make people angry.

Miss Elistine Connor was not the teacher to be pulling tricks on. She had a hot temper and the strength to back it up. Lowell made the mistake of targeting her as the victim of his tomfoolery once too often. She had him get up from his seat and march over to her desk. Then she gave him a thrashing he never forgot. But it did not stop his schoolroom antics. The entertainer in him was developing, causing him to "act" in front of a "captured audience"--the classroom.

The Thomas household was blessed with the birth of a baby daughter in 1904. She was given the name of Pherbia. Lowell wrote of his sister, "...there were twelve years between us, and I saw far too little of her."[14] Pherbia lived for seventy-seven years. She was a traveler in her later years. She wrote of her adventures and spoke for many societies. Pherbia's active life ended a few weeks before Lowell's in 1981.

James Warford was involved in the raid on the **Record** in 1903. On election day 1904, he killed two men in Goldfield. Chris Miller and Ike Liebo were constables of Precinct 48. In the morning hours, they were sitting on a fence outside of Miller's home. The house was across the street from the precinct's polling place.

Around 11 A.M., Deputy Warford found Miller and Liebo and ordered the men to move on. A few foul words were spat back and forth, then a gun battle ensued. Neither Miller nor Liebo fired a lethal shot. Warford's aim was deadly accurate.

Mrs. Miller saw the incident. She ran out of the house, picked up her husband's gun, and chased after Warford. He fled.

Both Miller and Liebo were wounded in their chests. The bullets had passed through their bodies and cut apart their spinal cords. Drs. Thomas, Driscoll, and Jones attended the men. Miller died not long after foray. Liebo held on for a few hours. In the afternoon, the bodies of the two men were moved to Dunn Undertaking.

Miller and Liebo had been union men. Chris Miller had been injured in the labor riot of 6 June 1903. Both had been deported in that same month. They returned to the district in October.

Warford claimed the shooting was self-defense. His past troubles with the labor union were too obvious to be coincidental. He was convicted of second degree murder.

Two years later, James Warford was living in Independence after serving a term at the state penitentiary in Canon City. Warford always carried his ivory-handled revolvers, but he did not look for trouble. One day in April 1906, Warford's mangled body was found near the main Portland shaft. Dr. Thomas, as city physician, performed the autopsy on the body. He stated in his report that fifteen bullet holes had pierced the chest and abdomen. The head had been cracked open, and the heart mutilated. The murder of Warford went unsolved.

11 November 1904: a fire engulfed Nelson's Grocery Store in Anaconda. The volunteer fire department speedily answered the alarm. They were not able to contain it. Within minutes, the fire had a firm hold on both sides of Main Street. The old wooden buildings were very close together. The fire consumed them like kindling.

Ten bulidings were destroyed. Insurance premiums had been so high on the old structures that few carried any kind of protection policy. Damage was estimated to be over $50,000. Most of the three hundred people who had lived in the town moved to Victor or Cripple Creek.

7 December: Dr. Cohen announced plans to take over the entire second floor of the Physicians' Building, converting it into the Emergency Hospital. Dr. Thomas and Dr. Latimer had to look for new offices.

George Kyner changed the overall outlook of the **Record**. His paper turned pro-mine owner. Three thousand dollars and new printing equipment from the Mine Owners Association had influenced Kyner's business opinions.

For the year 1904, the **Record** reported gold production to be $22,422,680.

1905

Dr. Thomas did not have to move his office very far. His equipment was taken from the southwest corner of Fourth and Victor Avenue to the southeast corner. He rented two rooms on the second floor of the building owned by the Central Drug Company. Carlton's City Bank was directly across the street. The **Record** office was only a stone's throw down South Fourth.

Reports from around the district opened the new year with enthusiasm.

J.M. Wright of Cripple Creek paid $160,000 for the Jo Dandy Mine on Raven Hill. An ore washing machine was installed. A few months after Wright purchasd the mine, a new ore body was discovered. It was eight to twelve feet in width and sported an average of four ounces of gold to the ton. The strike encouraged Wright's management to have every pound of ore sent through the wash.

The Woman's Club and New Century Club of Victor pooled their resources and sponsored a production of **As You Like It** on Wednesday, 1 February. George Sylvester and Florence Gale were the central actors. The stage was decorated with elaborate scenery, often changing for the various acts. Victor adored Shakespeare. The play was a glittering success.

Dr. Thomas was one of the founders of the New Century Club. His taste in literature made him a natural for the part. Father Downey, an Irish whiskey-drinking humanitarian, was also involved in forming the literary club. Mrs. Thomas played an active role in the Woman's Club, and helped establish the Shakespeare Club. Between the Thomases, Father Downey, the Kyners, Latimers, Cunninghams, and other intellectual leaders of the community, Victor was transformed into a cultural mining town.

The district was not to recover completely from the labor war. A criminal element, attracted by the violence of the strike, remained in the area. Once this criminal faction realized the potential of the district, it was determined to root itself into the business structure. When these hoodlums could not embezzle, highgrade, swindle, con, or "salt" mines, they occasionally resorted to common robbery.

The Silver Bell Saloon in Independence was run by Edward Fay and Henry Drech. At 9:45 P.M. on 11 February, when the saloon on Montgomery Street was doing a fair amount of business, two men intruded upon the premises. One of the men was Bill Dugan. The other was John Howell. Dugan carried a Winchester 38-40 poised for action. Howell was ready with his 38-calibre revolver. The two ruffians demanded tobacco and liquor. They were loading up their booty when Frank Edmundson, a patron of the saloon, charged out of the billiard room swinging a cue. The battle began.

Bill Gleason and H.L. Potts had been sitting at a table quietly drinking. They suddenly drew out their 38-calibre Colt revolvers and fired at the hooligans. Howell shot down Edmundson. Henry Drech bolted for the back door. Dugan's Winchester cut him down.

William Butt was standing in the doorway of the saloon with his hands raised when Marshal Charles Webster barged in. Edward Fay was shot before Webster could draw out his guns. Webster attacked with an eight-shot 38-calibre Colt automatic and a six-shot 38-calibre Colt revolver. The marshal trapped Dugan and Howell between himself and Gleason and Potts. Eight guns were blasting away at once.

Dugan was the first of the rascallions to be felled. After he hit the dirty wood floor, Howell attempted a wild escape through the billiard room. Tobacco flew all about as liquor bottles shattered on the hard floor. Webster emptied his Colt automatic into Howell. The desperado collapsed in a lifeless mass of blood, flesh, tobacco, and alcohol.

Twelve men had been in the saloon. Five were sprawled out on the floor. All guns were empty. Henry Drech died two days after the five-minute battle. Edward Fay lingered for two weeks before he succumbed to his wounds. Frank Edmundson recovered after surgery and some weeks of convalescence.

Bill Dugan had worked in the Gold Sovereign Mine. In 1896, he had made $40,000 in the Klondike. He lost it all shortly thereafter. John Howell usually rode under the alias of R.F. Harris. Both men were wanted for the robbery of the Naufert Saloon in Elkton. Neither man survived the gun battle in the Silver Bell.

On Valentine's Day, the Woman's Club entertained their husbands and sweethearts in the New Century Club. The parlors of the Baptist Church, on the corner of South Fourth and Portland Avenue, were lavishly decorated in red and white crepe paper. Streamers dangled all about and strings with hearts attached to their ends hung from the ceiling. In the dining room, the Woman's Club's colors, white and gold, were seen in the bouquets of carnations and daffodils. One large, ornate heart covered the east wall of the dining room.

A musical program was presented after dinner. Mrs. George Kyner sang a group of songs in the holiday mood. Then the men were given some sport. Each had to take a bow in hand and launch an arrow at the hearts of fortune. The marksmanship was atrocious, but prizes were awarded nonetheless.

Dr. Thomas gave the toast for the evening. Following which, he presented an enjoyable talk on the subject of "Our Wives". Dr. Thomas' delivery was highly entertaining, performed "in a humorous and witty manner".*

In the 5 March Sunday edition of the **Record** details of the New Century Club were listed. "The club has a membership of 25 composed principally of professional men, and prominent educators of the district, and has a high intellectual standing. The club meets every two weeks and the program of the evening consists of a round table, reading a paper on some important subject and discussion of the paper by members...."

The anniversary issue of the Victor **Daily Record** came out on 16 March. One section of the issue concerned itself with a report on the progress made in the Jo Dandy Mine. Averaging forty tons of two-ounce ore per day, the mine had already yielded $320,000. Some of the ore assayed out as high as fifty ounces of gold to the ton.

Late in the evening of 31 March, the electric Low Line rolled into Victor. Snow was piled on and around the tracks, causing difficulty for the engineer. On Seventh Street and Portland Avenue, the tram's front catcher picked up a heavy, dark mass. The snow-covered load was pushed along the track for several blocks but would not break up. The engineer stopped the tram.

Upon inspecting the mass, the engineer realized he had picked up more than snow. The load was actually the body of a man, still alive and overtly intoxicated. The engineer recruited help, and the man was taken to Dr. Cohen's Emergency Hospital. The drunk woke up the next morning. Suffering a few bruises and a cut over one eye, the man thought he was still en route to another bar. He had to be calmed when informed that the hospital did not serve liquor.

Jay Herold lived at 509 West Portland Avenue. Jay's father, J.J. Herold, worked at the Morrell Hardware Company. In the city election of 1905, J.J. Herold won the office of alderman of the Second Ward. James B. Cunningham, relative of S.G. Cunningham, was elected mayor. Lowell was exposed to the inner workings of politics when he visited Jay at his home. Political discussions were prevalent in the Herold house. J.J. Herold was not all that influential, but Victor was small enough that an alderman had access to much of the political machine.

Lowell learned from these visits that it was often wise to play a background part in politics. The figure in the front row had to express too many opinions. Lowell preferred to keep his opinions private. Throughout his journalism career, he remained a neutral figure to improve his objectivity. His nonopinionated stance helped him to retain his public for nearly a half century.

Lowell and Jay liked football and girls better than politics. Lucille McAvoy lived at 223 South Sixth Street, only a few houses away from Lowell. The McAvoy house had three stories and a barn. Lowell liked Lucille, as did nearly all the other boys in the school. The McAvoy porch was always lined with Lucille's admirers. Room for Lowell and Jay was sparse.

At a birthday party at Lucille's house, the game of postoffice was introduced. This was done in the barn when her parents were not chaperoning. Lowell had just turned thirteen and was eager to try out this new game. Only, he wanted to play it with Lucille. As it turned out, he was paired with a girl named Bessie. One kiss from her made him forget about Lucille.

Lowell and Dale Latimer were called an "item" at one time. Dale's father was Dr. Latimer. Lowell and Dale were really nothing more than friends, but they played along with their classmates when it was convenient. There was an occasion in McAvoy's barn when he and Dale were persuaded to go up into the hayloft. Amongst the warm, dusty hay, Lowell and Dale sat three feet apart from each other. They did not even dare to touch hands. They let the others believe what they wanted.

Samuel Vidler, the newspaper correspondent and broadswordsman, was in the headlines 13 April. Sam and his wife had separated in February. He started seeing Mrs. Helen Coulter Douglas of Colorado City. Mrs Mattie Vidler heard of the liaison and could not contain her grief. At nine in the morning, Mattie went over to the Denver **Republican** newspaper office in Cripple Creek and drew out Sam's pay. Then she bought herself a 38-calibre revolver and two boxes of cartridges.

Helen Douglas was a divorcee. She was an attractive woman: brunette, dark brown eyes, oval face, five-foot-six-inches tall. Mattie located Sam and Helen in Room 336 of the National Hotel. When Mattie knocked on the door, Helen answered in her nightgown. Sam, partially dressed, ran for the closet. Mattie aimed her revolver at Helen and fired. The bullet entered Helen's body just under her left nipple. She gasped once and died.

Mattie remained at the scene of the murder. She quietly submitted to arrest. Later, she was released on $5,000 bond. In the trial of 12 May, Mattie Vidler was acquitted of first degree murder. Attorney Tom C. Brown had successfully defended her on a case of temporary insanity.

Sam and Mattie Vidler were reunited.

Members of the Law and Order League pressured city officials into "cleaning up" Victor. In May, the tenderloin was infiltrated by police raids. Arrests were made for everything from public drunkenness to illicit cohabitation.

But the city profited from prostitution. A monthly charge of sixteen dollars was levied on all madams running parlour houses. Plus, they paid six dollars for every girl they employed. This dissuaded the police from arresting very many of the "soiled doves". 18 May, the **Record** reported, "Hardly a night passes when the police are not called to settle one row or another (in the tenderloin), and it has become so regular that they are going to put a damper on the whole thing." The "damper" was a feather dropped upon a deluge of alcohol.

Lowell was a popular boy in school. His classroom antics brought him the attention he wanted, but they usually landed him in trouble. The reactions from his teachers also "emphasized" his presence--another of his desired effects. He was a natural entertainer.

When the eighth grade class graduated at the end of May, Miss Elistine Connor could not have been more pleased. Lowell was one of the most intelligent children in the class. Yet, his unpredictable outbursts made teaching a difficult task. After the graduation picnic, she thought she had heard the last from Lowell.

"The eighth grade graduating class had a picnic at Eureka gulch Thursday afternoon, chaperoned by Miss Connor and Mr. Burton. The best kind of a time was enjoyed by the jolly crowd of boys and girls. Good things to eat were in abundance and the appetites phenomenal."* Many of Lowell's friends, whom he would know through all of his school years in Victor, were present: Anna Bullock, Homer Huffaker, Emalene Jones, Gertrude Lamb, Edna Neuman, John Pascoe, Leslie Schoen, and Harold Worcester.

11 July: the Gentry Brothers Famous Shows United made a spectacular appearance amongst the richest gold mines of Colorado. A long list of circus acts filled a page in the **Record.** The show was billed as "A Beautiful array of Beautiful Magnificence." Performances included the Norman Family as acrobats and Indian club jugglers; the Yohasmite Japanese Troupe, masters of the martial arts; two hundred performing horses and dogs, fifty monkey comedians, and a troop of musical ponies. The most unique sights were three performing elephants, a camel and its baby.

At 10:30 A.M., a street parade along Victor Avenue drew the crowds in. Clowns excited the children. The performers intrigued the parents. Lowell and Jay were not able to resist this spectacular.

As the **Record** became the most circulated paper in Teller County, the Kyners' social popularity grew. Mrs. Kyner was in demand for her singing. George Kyner, as a "mouthpiece" for the mine owners, was accepted by A.E. Carlton's group. But their rising social status did not make them immune to misfortune.

12 July: the Kyner house was burglarized. The house was broken into through the kitchen window. Police investigation determined there may have been as many as three thieves. The heist was interrupted by the 10:45 P.M. arrival of the boarder residing in the Kyner house. A lady's gold watch and a small sum of money were stolen. Mrs. Kyner had been singing at the Methodist Church, which accounted for the Kyners' absence.

18 August: a blast reverberated in Victor. An ore sorter from the Portland Mine, Orman C. Smith, age 44, was at his home, 108 North Seventh Street. He had been ill for nearly two weeks and was under the care of a physician. Orman had lived in Victor for nine years. He had few acquaintances. For some unexplained reason, he was working with dynamite in his home. At seven in the morning, an explosion shook North Seventh Street.

Upon the arrival of Fire Chief O'Neill and the city coroner, Orman was found dead. His head had been blown off. Bits of hair and brains were clinging to the walls and ceiling. The badly disfigured body was carried to the Victor Undertaking Company, 204 Victor Avenue. It was never learned whether the blast was accidental or intentional.

By the end of August, Lowell had to start looking forward to the ninth grade. He was already going to the Victor High School since the building held the eighth through twelfth grades. D.P. Taylor was to be the principal during the coming school year. Lowell was alarmed to find out that he and Miss Elistine Connor would share classrooms again.

Classes did not begin until after Labor Day. The celebration for this year was designed to show the state and the country that the Cripple Creek-Victor Mining District was back on its feet again. The Thomases had spent the weekend of 26 August in Colorado Springs, but they were not about to miss the festivities planned for Victor.

The Elks were backing most of the holiday celebrations, and had arranged the lion's share of the activities. Cripple Creek was still gun-shy; they let Victor risk the large crowds. But the Cripple Creek businessmen threw in their monetary support.

The parade started at ten in the morning. It began on South Third Street, turned left at the first intersection, and continued down the full length of Victor Avenue. The Colorado National Guard and the Knights of Pythias led the procession. Second to march were representatives of the mines, starting in alphabetical order--from the Ajax to the Zoe. This entailed over two hundred active properties. The children of Washington, Garfield, and Lincoln were next in line. The Woodmen of the World, Modern Woodmen, and Royal Neighbors followed. The McGee Mercantile Cornet Band and Pioneers of 1891 marched behind them. Carriages holding citizens and officials of the city government rolled up next. The fire department marched ahead of the floats and other rigs.

Rain blanketed most of the day's activities. Yet, thousands endured to watch the proceedings. The award for the best float was given to the Victor Wigwam of Red Men and Ladies of Pocahontas. First prize for the most detailed carriage was awarded to the Victor **Daily Record**. The Victor Lodge of Elks No. 367 and the Victor Eagles marched togehter in "Prince Albert" regalia for the parade's grand finale.

A great many events were held throughout the day. Lowell participated in the three-hundred-yard burro race for boys under fourteen years of age. He did not win first place, but he enjoyed the competition.

The drilling contest was a mining town specialty. Victor prided itself on staging them every chance it could. Contestants had to possess Mine Owners Association cards and work in a mine in the district. Piston drills exceeding two-and-a-quarter inches could not be used. The drill had to be mounted on a tripod. The hose was required to be three-fourths of an inch in diameter and the steel drill bit seven to eight inches long. All holes drilled had to be four inches deep, except for the last.

Fair competition was of utmost importance. Cussing out loud was not permitted and resulted in immediate disqualification. A ten-dollar entrance fee was mandatory. This was usually paid by the mining or manufacturing company the contestant represented. A one-hundred-dollar prize was a awarded for the fastest setup, and a hundred-and-fifty-dollar prize for the greatest amount of holes drilled to the deepest extent. Six hundred dollars was raised by the contest for the miners' fund.

Many people were "fined" during the day to help raise money for the permanently injured miners of the Independence Depot incident. Charges against those "fined" were heard in a "kangaroo court." Fines were handed out for talking to one's wife, walking, sneezing, and cussing. Reverend Lansdell was fined for preaching in public.

Platform dances were held as part of the celebration. At night, there was dancing at McCarville's Hall, 508-510 Victor Avenue. A masked ball was underway at 8 P.M. on Fourth and Victor Avenue. The streets were decorated with strings of colored lights. And a carnival along with fireworks ended the day's festivities.

Some 3,800 tourists rode up on the trains to be a part of Victor's Labor Day Celebration. "I looked forward to holidays like the Fourth of July and Labor Day as though they were my birthday, for then all the barely constrained excitement of the gold camp burst into dawn-to-dawn celebration--fireworks, prize fights, hard-rock drilling contests and rodeos, each with its favorites and heroes."[15] Lowell found these celebrations to be alive with people. No other subject besides adventure was as interesting to him.

V. Lee Bostder, age 35, worked in the Gold Sovereign Mine. On 1 October, he was loading a huge ore bucket to be hoisted from the ninth level to the surface. F.R. Snyder was standing about five feet from Bostder. Without warning, the cable of the bucket snapped. 1,500 pounds of ore fell ninety-five feet and landed on top of Bostder. He was "crushed to atoms."*

5 October: the Mable M. shaft of the Gold Dollar Mine was being worked by the Milwaukee Mutual Company. At a depth of six hundred and thirty-nine feet, a streak of pure sylvanite and calaverite cubes were uncovered. The vein was a half-inch across. The assay value was 1,468 ounces of gold per ton, or $29,360.

5 October: the "Shakespeare Club held a profitable meeting at the home of Mrs. Hattie Bourk on South Fourth Street."* Officers were elected, and Mrs. Lansdell was voted president. Mrs. Harriet Thomas, Mrs. Hattie Worcester, and Mrs. Amelia McFarland were also elected as officers at the Thursday night meeting.

9 October: the Victor Opera House staged **The Forbidden Land.** The mystery in the title fascinated Lowell. The book by Guy F. Steely focused on what little was known about the country of Tibet. The lead role was played by Edward Garvie. Music was composed by Frederic Chapin.

The phrase "forbidden land" held a certain magnetism for Lowell. Crossing "forbidden" borders became one of his life's quests. In 1921-22, he arranged a trip into the country of Afghanistan.

"Three 'forbidden' lands, for us of the West, lie in Asia. The first is 'Holy Arabia,' the region of the sacred Mohammedan cities of Mecca and Medina. The second is Tibet, far up on the 'roof of the world,' the meeting-place of the winds of earth, where his Serene Highness the Dalai Lama, 'the reincarnation of the Buddha,' rules over the warrior monks who dwell in vast monasteries on the rocky summits of the Himalaya. The third is the land of another mighty range, the Hindu Kush, south of the Oxus River and beyond the northwest frontier of India-- Afghanistan. The door is the Khyber Pass...."[16]

Afghanistan was a lawless country sealed off from the rest of the world by its ruler, customs, and politics. Because it was "forbidden" to travel into Afghanistan, Lowell had to do it.

A great deal of ambassadorial action was needed to obtain permission. The mystery was a strong enough lure for Lowell's adventurous spirit. His energetic cleverness and will-power accomplished the task.

In 1949, Lowell and Lowell Thomas, Jr. embarked on yet another of their adventures into "forbidden lands". The country was Tibet. "I have always presumed that growing up on a mountaintop had something to do with this insatiable craving to go places. As a boy, from our vantage point high in the Colorado Rockies, I could see in the distance the beckoning snow-capped peaks of the Snagre de Cristo range and sense the world's breadth. Ever since then I have been irresistibly drawn toward the farthest horizons."[17]

Lowell and his son were the seventh and eighth Americans ever granted permission to enter Tibet and travel to its wondrous capital city, Lhasa. Both he and his son looked upon their journey as one of the highlights of their careers. Lowell Thomas, Jr. was so impressed by the privilege of touring this "forbidden land" that he devoted three books to the adventure: **The Silent War In Tibet, The Dalai Lama,** and **Out of This World.**

The Victor Opera House put on other absorbing plays in October. One of these was Channing Pollock's adaptation of Frank Norris' **The Pit.** The novel was converted into four acts and six scenes. Wilton Lackaye played the leading role. **The Pit** was called "A great symphony of American life."* The play was promoted as a spectacle: "See the Big Panic Scene in the Chicago Wheat Pit".*

Frank Norris, a naturalistic novelist, also wrote **The Octopus,** a story of the railroads' monopoly of California transportation. Norris was purportedly working on a novel about Victor when he died in 1902.

At the end of October, the **Record** was proud to report that $2,112.60 had been accrued for the injured miners of the Independence Depot catastrophe.

The **Record** was also pleased to report the strike in the Bill Nye claim on Copper Mountain. One hundred and eighty-five feet down and ninety feet from the main shaft, on the lease of the Metallic Gold Mining Company, a five-foot wide vein of black tellurium was unearthed. The ore contained nine hundred and sixty-five ounces of gold and two hundred and forty-six ounces of silver to the ton. The gold was found in both sylvanite and calaverite forms. A ton of ore was worth $19,300.

26 October: "The Shakespeare Club, which at its organization, planned to hold a special meeting every fourth Thursday of the month when the husbands and sweethearts of members were to be entertained, gave a Halloween party Thursday night at the home of Miss Elistine Connor at the Cooper Home on West Victor Avenue. For fun and genuine merriment the affair has seldom been equaled."*

Preparations and decorations were given the utmost attention. Menacing ghosts and flickering jack-o-lanterns greeted guests walking up to the front verandah. The reception room was filled with Halloween colors and symbols. Each guest was given an attractive pumpkin flower to wear throughout the evening. After the vice-president of the club, Mrs. D.P. Taylor, gave an opening talk, the guests were entertained with fortune-telling.

A large, black-painted witch hung on a wall. Fortune cards were pinned to it. A guest was blindfolded and sent to select a card of fate. After all the guests had chosen cards and a great deal of enjoyment was had in sharing each other's fate, other games ensued. The last one before dinner was one of walnut shells. Names on pieces of paper were placed in the shells and hidden all over the house. Every guest had to find a shell so he would know where he was to sit at the dinner table.

Among the guests were the Eads, Bourks, Eastons, Murrays, McFarlands, McGarrys, Meeks, Strains, Taylors, Worcesters, and the Thomases. Miss Elistine Connor had some enlightening tales to relate to Dr. and Mrs. Thomas about their son's boisterous shenanigans.

Phillip Herrington was single-jacking in the Granite Mine on 9 November. He had just finished dislodging a large section of ore. Bringing up his wheelbarrel, he began hauling away some of the loose rocks. Fifteen feet above his head, an eight-to-ten-ton slab of rock gave way. It fell flat on top of Herrington. After the tonnage was removed by rescuers, the body of Phillip Herrington was found crushed to a pulp.

10 November: warnings were issued by Sheriff Edward Bell that all saloons, drugstores, cigarstores, newsstands, stationery stores, dance halls, and gambling houses were banned from running dice games, slot machines, or any other kind of sporting device. As part of this new decree, all saloons were to be closed on Saturday at midnight. They were not to reopen until Monday morning. Along with saloons, all cribs and houses of ill-fame were also to be closed on Sundays. Theaters were asked to comply with this ruling.

On Sunday, 12 November, the theaters ignored the will of Sheriff Bell and the Law and Order League. No further legal actions were taken.

13 November: Victor was sparkling with awe. An ice cave had been discovered in Cow Mountain. South of Bison Park and two miles from the railroad, the ice palace was excavated by two miners. Upon exploration, the ice was measured to be eighteen inches thick in the first room. In the next part of the cave, a small lake had been formed. The ceiling was a dazzling frescoe of frost and ice. The third room was located at the bottom of a one-hundred-and-fifty-foot frozen waterfall. Below the waterfall was another lake. Its size was incalculable. The water was a lush dark blue.

The men who discovered the ice cave were thinking of installing electric lights and turning it into a summer resort like the Cave of the Winds in Manitou Springs.

21 November: Mrs. Maggie Morrison, described as "fair, fat, and forty of Independence"* was arrested. She was riding the Short Line to Colorado Springs. Mrs. Morrison, a boarding housekeeper, had one hundred and twenty-five pounds of high-grade ore in her seven *grips* (luggage). A "go-between" for a gang of highgraders, Mrs. Morrison's haul was worth $10,000.

Victor had that "irresistible combination of a no-questions-asked frontier town and the chance to strike it rich, that lured a gaudy cross section of humanity"[18] into its golden realm. Human interest stories were everywhere. "They were not difficult to gather in mining-town journalism. In the old gold and silver camps life was all too human and violently interesting."[19] Lowell absorbed it all and became a part of it himself.

Production for 1905 was reported by the **Record** to be $23,757,952.

A.E. Carlton's City Bank Building. This building has been the home of many businesses throughout the years. Up until 4 November 1903, it was the Woods' First National Bank of Victor. The banking facilities were on the first floor. Dr. Thomas once rented an office in this building for his medical practice. In the middle of the Twentieth Century, the building became the Victor Hotel. Today, it is vacant.

1906

"Every woman should insist that their husbands buy a bottle of our wholesome, Pure Whiskey, it never fails to cure a cold." This introduction to a liquor ad placed in the **Record** must have given the ladies in the Shakespeare Club a hearty laugh. The medicinal plea, though typical of patent medicines of the period, was as ancient and fallacious as love potions. Besides, the author's grammar was a bit awkward.

Mrs. Thomas and the other women in the Shakespeare Club met at Miss Carrie Brunson's house in January. **Taming of the Shrew** was the first play discussed, then the group proceeded to **Julius Caesar.**

January saw the intriguing production of **Faust** at the Victor Opera House. But in February, Mephisto summoned up another kind of hell on the 1,350 foot level of the Blue Bird Mine. Allen Webster, Fred Harvey, and James Stevens had been lowered through the main shaft at 8 A.M. Stevens traveled back up with the cage, and then Tollak Olson and W.P. Guzman went down. Eleven hundred feet through the shaft, Olson and Guzman were overcome by carbonic acid gas. Olson collapsed, rolled out of the cage, and fell two hundred and fifty feet to the bottom of the shaft.

Allen Webster succumbed to the gas on the thirteenth level of the mine. Fred Harvey tried dragging Webster towards the cage when he began to suffocate. A rescue team was alerted. When they arrived, Webster, Harvey, and Guzman were placed on the cage. While it was being hoisted up, Fred Benjamin of the rescue party collapsed and started to fall off the platform. Benjamin's pelvis was crushed between the cage and the shaft.

On the surface, the five injured men were rushed to the Red Cross hospital. Webster, Olson, and Benjamin died.

9 February: both Dr. Thomas and Lowell made some delightful news. "Dr. H.G. Thomas visited the high school recently and gave a very interesting and instructive talk on the subject of vaccination. He gave an excellent account of its discovery and showed the great benefit which had resulted from it." Then, "The Socratic Debating Society holds its meetings in the assembly room on Friday evenings at 7:45. The club recently elected Frank Cunningham as president and Lowell Thomas as secretary...The annual oratorical contest is to be held next Friday evening. The boys are working hard on this and it promises to be the most closely contested in the history of the school. The proceeds are to go to the athletic association."

Lowell was thirteen and in the ninth grade. It was obviously true that he was "the lucky beneficiary of" his father's "insatiable quest for knowledge."[20] Both of the male Thomases practiced their belief that "Your voice is the expression of your personality."[21] Because of his father's learning, Lowell was grades ahead of his fellow students.

His position as secretary in the debating society linked him to Frank Cunningham. Frank was related to the manager of the opera house, Stephen Cunningham. Tickets to any performance at the theater were within Lowell's grasp.

10 February: one of the most gruesome cases of insurance fraud in Victor's history was solved. 22 January 1906, Jack J. McEachern was working his lease of the Three Jacks Tunnel on Straub Mountain. Jack Varley, alias Jack Crowley the prize-fighter, was working with McEachern. Varley was supposedly in a nearby cabin thawing powder when an explosion at the tunnel occurred. What little was left of McEachern was moved to the Victor Undertaking Company. Funeral services were held at the Catholic church.

Marshal Naylor of Victor was suspicious about the case. He discovered during his investigation that McEachern had recently been insured for over $11,000 by three separate companies. Even more current, McEachern had tried to purchase additional insurance from the Northwestern Mutual Life Insurance Company, but was turned down.

Marshal Naylor asked questions of Coroner Gessell and George Hall of the Victor Undertaking Company. Naylor then inspected the Three Jacks Tunnel. The largest part of McEachern's body that had been found was a six-inch section of leg. Body pieces had been scattered over a twenty-foot radius. The head of the body had been distorted beyond recognition. A thought lodged itself in Naylor's mind: not a trace of blood had been found.

He could not rationalize this odd scrap of information. Then a very conclusive piece of evidence came to light. Strands of hair picked up in the blast vicinity were found to be brown and straight. McEachern's hair had been red and curly.

The facts were hurled back together by Naylor. A man named Robert Speed, who had been killed in a mining accident in the Portland two days before McEachern's ''death'', had been buried in Sunnyside Cemetery on 21 January. Naylor received permission to dig up Speed's grave. Reaching the six foot level, Naylor uncovered what he had expected--nothing. Jack Varley was arrested. He confessed the entire plan.

Marshal Naylor rode to 500 1/2 South Second Street with warrants. Mrs. McEachern and her three children were gone. 10 February: Jack McEarchern was arrested. He was convicted of insurance fraud and grave robbery. The remains of Robert Speed were laid to rest for the second time.

Harry Orchard was arrested for dynamiting ex-Governor Frank Steunenberg of Idaho. Once in jail, Orchard confessed to all sorts of crimes he had committed in the name of the Western Federation of Miners. Bill Haywood, Charles Moyer, and George Pettibone were implicated in many of the wrongdoings.

In some ways, the people of Victor were relieved by Orchard's confessions. Many of the crimes that had occurred during the recent labor war were, solved. But in other ways, people were shocked. For two years, criminals thought of as lawful citizens had been walking free in the streets of Victor.

Saturday, 24 February: "One of the notable social functions of the week was the special meeting of the Shakespeare Club, which was held last evening at Masonic Hall, when the members entertained their husbands and several other guests most royally. The committee in whose hands the arrangements were placed are to be most heartily congratulated on the success which crowned their efforts. The hall was tastefully decorated in the club colors, lavender and white, and the club flower, the violet, was painted in water colors on the programs, the skillful work of Miss Colby, while the club motto was printed on the programs very artistically by Mrs. Worcester and consists of the following quotation:

'Find tongues in hills,
Books in running brooks,
Sermons in stones, and
Good in everything.'

"The tableaus were taken from the plays the Club has studied during the winter and were most successfully given. The vocal and instrumental solos were well rendered."* The entertainments were an instrumental solo by Miss Kennedy, a scene from **Julius Caesar** where Mrs. Wilson played Brutus and Miss Copley played Portia, and a quartette of Mesdames Murray and Thomas, Misses Connor and Copley, all singing "I Know A Bank."

"After the program a banquet was served, the guests selecting partners by matching cards of Shakespearean quotations. Dr. Thomas was the clever toast master."* The Shakespeare and New Century clubs were more than social organizations. They were centers of learning and culture. They were also places where Dr. Thomas could display his humorous and entertaining oratory skills.

Lowell's love and admiration for his father was so strong that he emulated him in many ways. Characteristics such as humor, oratorical skills, love for learning, philanthropy, a penchant for talk, superb memory, and objective outlook were all adapted by Lowell. One of the major differences between him and his father was the fact that Lowell was still young enough to be effected by Victor's powerful charisma and personality. This effect converted the characteristics he had adapted from his father into an active wanderlust for adventure.

Victor was gold. Working in the mines changed Lowell's life forever. "And even later, when I would be called on to speak to black-tie audiences, I could always break the ice by telling them that I had gotten my start in an *ore house.*"22 His first job in the mines began in the summer of 1906.

He worked in the Empire State Mine. Its wealthy Buena Vein yielded $36,000 in gold for every ton of ore. He was placed on pick and shovel labor, loading up the ore cars and pushing them to the main shaft. The work was hard, but listening to the miners speak of far away places sent Lowell's imagination on a thousand different journeys throughout the world.

Victor had a heart of gold in more ways than one. When San Francisco was leveled by one of the most destructive earthquakes to hit an American city, the people of Victor were among the first to send aid. 19 April 1906, the day after the disaster, an informal challenge was inaugurated in the district. The object was to raise the most money possible to help San Francisco's recovery.

Victor took a strong lead immediately. In the first few days, it raised $1,345 while Cripple Creek, in second place, had only $772. By the end of April, Victor had sent over $4,220. The sums of all the other towns of the district added together did not equal that amount.

4 May: the senior class of the Victor High School staged their rendition of Shakespeare's **The Winter's Tale** at the Victor Opera House. Lowell, although he was only fourteen and in the ninth grade, was a member of the cast. Leontes was portrayed by Franklin J. Mannix. Willie Dodsworth played Mamillius. John Pascoe was Phocion. In all, there were twenty players in the cast. The Victor High School Orchestra provided music for the production.

Lowell was Father Time. A soliloquy, such as in the opening Act IV, Scene I, was perfect for Lowell's long-practiced oratorical skills:

> *Time.* "I, that please some, try all, both joy and terror
> Of good and bad, that makes and unfolds error,
> Now take upon me, in the name of Time,
> To use my wings...."

Lowell was a Shakespearean actor in Victor. His clear and deeply resonating tones were just forming into the voice that would be heard around the world for forty-six years. His style altered some by the time he started broadcasting for CBS and NBC on 29 September 1930:

> "Adolf Hitler, the German Fascist chief, is snorting fire. There are now two Mussolinis in the world, which seems to promise a rousing time. Adolf has written a book called the German Fascist Bible. In it this belligerent gentleman states that a cardinal policy of his now powerful German party is the conquest of Russia. That's a tall assignment, Adolf. You just ask Napoleon."[23]

The impetus for Lowell's witty style of delivery was Dr. Thomas' own style. Shakespeare may have helped to add concision and clarity to his voice. But he developed his own style from a synthesis of all he had learned. Lowell Thomas became the most listened-to man in the world.

In 1906, Lowell was involved in many social occasions. He participated in drama clubs. He attended parties. He played football and ran in track meets. He debated at the Socratic Society meetings. He went on geology hikes. He found a myriad of directions to channel his energetic personality. Before he was fourteen, he climbed Pike's Peak. It was evident that Lowell could not sit back and rest.

16 May: "Gertrude Lamb and Ruth Emens were charming young hostesses Thursday evening when they entertained. The party was given at the home of pupils of the high school, Miss Lamb's parents, Mr. and Mrs. A.W. Oliver (421 South Third Street) ...The entertainment was most delightful, reflecting distinction in the courtesy and hospitality of these young ladies. Carnations and ferns were used in the decorations."* Games such as "high five" and "free-for-all" were part of the evening. Lowell was one of the thirty young guests.

Lowell left the Empire State Mine to start work in the Tornado Mine. He carted ore out of a stope notorious for its falling rock. Lowell was a gentleman to the mythological "tommyknockers" who lived in the mines. He was fortunate never to be caught in a mining accident.

Throughout his years in the mines, Lowell worked as a "mucker, trammer, driller, ore sorter"[24] and assay rider. The one job he did not mind working was ore sorter.

> "...as you routinely sifted the various grades of rock you
> could listen to the gaudy tales of men who had been on
> the trail of gold in the farthest corners of earth, from the
> Klondike to South Africa. This experience had a marked
> effect on me. Only a few years later, when I had a chance
> to break away from the day-in, day-out routines of life, I
> too went off looking for adventure, and it was those ore-
> house stories that sent me to Alaska."[25]

The Alaskan adventures of 1914 and 1915, combined with his enthusiastic speaking skills were the initiation of his life-long career in journalism.

In 1916, Lowell was a student and a professor at Princeton. F. Scott Fitzgerald was a junior at the college, writing plays for the Triangle Club. Lowell gave shows on his Alaskan trips, highlighting them with films and exuberant talk. Secretary of the Interior Franklin K. Lane, under President Woodrow Wilson, was told of Lowell's presentations. Lowell was asked to speak to a conference of "western governors, congressmen, naturalists, and national parks superintendents"[26] at the Smithsonian Institute. The conference's purpose was to promote Lane's "See America First!" campaign.

In January 1917, Lowell rushed to New York. He located Dale Carnegey (Carnegie) to ask his assistance in preparing his talk for the conference. Lowell was a success. Lane offered him the job of director of his campaign. He accepted.

Lowell was twenty-one when America entered World War I. He thought he should go to Europe and cover the war before embarking on the "See America First!" project. Lane agreed. Lowell was on his way to "discovering" Lawrence of Arabia.

A grand recital was announced by the Woman's Club of Victor. The date was set for 13 September 1906. Hans Albert and Mrs. Kyner were to entertain. Hans Albert, once considered the "world's third greatest violinist",* had moved to Victor because of his asthmatic condition.

Albert was originally from Vienna. He had been the *Konzertmeister* of the Imperial Opera, appointed by the Emperor of Austria when he was only sixteen. At the age of nineteen, Albert was asked to play for President and Mrs. Grover Cleveland at the White House.

In America, Albert had experienced his first downfall. He became addicted to morphine and whiskey--a side effect of his treatment for asthma. Hans Albert was reduced to playing his violin in saloons for spare money. His worn-out clothes dangled from his five-foot-two-inch frame. His violin case was always in his arms. Albert had become a familiar, pathetic figure on Victor Avenue.

The night Victor Herbert's opera, **Mele Modiste,** was presented at the Victor Opera House, Albert's fate had been delegated an unexpected twist. The leading lady of the light opera was Fritzi Scheff. Her schedule was disrupted when her conductor suffered a mild heart attack on the way up to Victor. New arrangements had to be made quickly. The name of Hans Albert was suggested. Fritzi Scheff was impressed.

Albert accepted the baton of the fifteen-piece orchestra. Rarely had the Victor Opera House been treated to such a combination of musical talents as heard that night.

During the grande finale, the theater was darkened. Suspense was at its greatest. Albert's performance of beautiful improvisations of the opera's melodies filled the galleries. The audience was captivated. Applause for the show was vigorous. When Fritzi Scheff stepped to the footlights on the last ovation, she introduced Hans Albert and called him the truest of artists.

Hans Albert had been given new life. He was in demand all over the district. He and Mrs. Kyner performed superbly together, and often repeated their shows for various occasions. Albert played music such as: **Frolic of the Imps** by Bazzini, **Faust Fantasie** by Saraste, **Narcissus** by Nevin-Albert, and **Carmen Fantasie** by Saraste. Mrs. Kyner would sing: **Mio Fernando** by Donnizetti and **Winds in the Trees** by Goring-Thomas. Their recitals always attracted large, fashionable audiences.

But life was not always to be optimistic for Albert. Continued recurrences of asthma sent him back to whiskey and morphine, and ultimately to an asylum. He recovered again and was declared sane in 1907. He married his love, Miss Grace Hadsell, in September of 1908, and returned to Victor. The happiness they shared lasted only a few years before his addictions again destroyed his sanity.

In September 1906, Lowell was in the tenth grade. Mabel Barbee (Lee) became his most admired teacher. "She captivated me first--along with every other boy in class--with her cool good looks. Then, having fallen head over heels in love with her, I followed willingly as she led me into the magic of ancient and modern history, and through the complexities of Spanish grammar."[27]

Mabel Barbee was spellbound by Lowell. "One...lad in particular loomed as a continuous challenge to my meager knowledge of modern history. He was quiet-mannered and fine-looking, with dark wavy hair and serious (blue) eyes that seemed to see through my thin pretensions. He was a hard though silent taskmaster. Before long I was immersed in cramming my head with world history, fortifying myself against his unexpected questions."[28]

Lowell was correct in thinking Mabel Barbee a special teacher. After she married a Victor mining engineer, Howe Lee, she moved to Oregon. When Lee died, she moved back to Colorado and became dean of women at Colorado College. She eventually helped establish Bennington College in Vermont. Mabel Barbee Lee, with Lowell's aid, then became "to the Cripple Creek gold camp what Bret Harte was to the California of the forty-niners and what Jack London and Robert Service were to the Klondike gold rush, unofficial historian of an epic."[29] Her books, **Cripple Creek Days** and **Return to Cripple Creek** were best sellers.

Mabel Barbee Lee described Lowell as being "quiet-mannered." He must have been showing her some favoritism. His school record depicted him as something of a wisecracker and prankster.

In another of his tenth grade classes, Lowell emoted a loud, sarcastic remark about the teacher's name. The man was called Mr. Lady. Lowell's remark was a pun on the man's name. He did not get away with his foolishness. He believed he set "a Victor High record for corporal punishment for a single offense."[30]

Mr. Lady was adept at other things besides math. He gave Lowell a good thrashing before the class, then sent him to the principal. The principal was occupied with other matters, so Lowell was sent home. There, Dr. Thomas gave him a beating for his remark. Back at school the next day, the principal was informed of Lowell's classroom antics. Lowell received another thrashing.

Between trouble, work, and study, Lowell parceled out some time to practice with the high school football team. Practice was every afternoon. The field was a vacant lot on South Fourth Street between Spicer and Portland avenues. Coach Craig and his assistant, Mr. Caley, trained the boys to run and think quickly. Football, in this period, was a game composed mostly of running, kicking, and passing.

The average weight of the Victor High School football team was one hundred and thirty-nine pounds. William Hayes was quarterback and captain. Parks Van Dolah was center. Harry Black played left halfback; Ray Shaw, right halfback. Leonard Hart was the fullback and a boy named Dugan was left guard. Lowell Thomas played left tackle; Joe Brill, right tackle.

"Miss Electa Franklin entertained a few of her friends last Saturday informally but most pleasantly. Dominoes was the amusement of the evening. Mr. Chas Eby being the lucky winner of the prize, a handsome picture. After the games dainty refreshments were served by the young hostess. The guests were: Lucile McAvoy, Dale Latimer, Edna Neuman, Harry Schlendering, Lowell Thomas, Charles Eby, and John Pascoe."* Electa's father was the general manager of the Eagle Ore Sampler Company. He had twice been the mayor of Victor. The Franklins lived in a beautiful home at 410 Lee Avenue.

Chancellor Henry A. Buchtel of the University of Denver ran for the office of Governor of Colorado in 1906. He spoke at the Victor Opera House on 30 October. The 1,200 seats of the theater were hastily filled. Hundreds of people had to stand in the aisles. Special trains from Goldfield, Independence, and Cripple Creek arrived minutes before Buchtel's 7:30 P.M. speech.

The main theme of his speech was "I want to see labor and capitol get along together, we need them both."* People believed he would clean up the state's political machine. Buchtel was elected governor.

Lowell enrolled in classes at the University of Denver in the fall of 1912. He already had two degrees from the University of Northern Indiana. Henry Buchtel was again chancellor of the University of Denver. Lowell consulted Buchtel personally about the classes he should take. After sharing stories about Victor, Lowell ended up enrolling in both undergraduate and graduate courses.

He held down part-time jobs as a reporter for the Rocky Mountain **News** and the Denver **Times** while attending classes. He also became acquainted with Gene Fowler of **The Denver Post.** Fowler was destined to be one of William Randolph Hearst's prize editors, and a successful Hollywood script writer. Lowell graduated from the University of Denver in 1914.

6 November 1906: The Victor High School football team won over Cripple Creek. The game was played in two halves: the first being twenty-five minutes long; and the second, twenty minutes. A total of one hundred and fifty students watched the game.

The night of the victory was more dazzling than the game itself. A bonfire was built by the students near the Victor High School. Rockets were launched and other fireworks tossed about. Following this, fifty students dressed in nightshirts and pillowcases marched through Victor "whooping their heads loose"* all the way. The entire affair spelled out Lowell's kind of entertainment.

At the home of Homer Huffaker, 415 Spicer Avenue, a book carnival was held on Wednesday, 26 December. All the young guests came dressed in costumes which represented their favorite books. The Huffaker house was decorated in Christmas colors. Strands of evergreen with red bells lined the interior. Guessing the book each guest represented was the highlight of the occasion. Books and writing paper were given away as prizes.

The most admired costumes were those of Electa Franklin, representing **Paradise Lost,** and Gertrude Lamb, as **Our Mutual Friend.** Other guests included Edna Neuman, Joe Brill, Ray Shaw, Harry Black, Leonard Hart, and Lowell Thomas.

Gertrude Lamb (Oliver) was of special interest to Lowell. To him, she acted and appeared more mature than the other girls in the school. These characteristics impressed him. When he showed her special attention she reacted favorably. Soon, he was at her home, 421 South Third, as often as possible.

Lowell's visits were lengthy. A ringing alarm clock lowered over the second floor railing by Mr. Oliver often ended their visits. Mr. Oliver was a jovial man. His actions were meant in the best of humor.

After one of these long stays, Lowell was walking up Lee Avenue towards his house on South Sixth when he heard footsteps from behind. He turned around. Mr. Oliver looked at him straight in the face. Lowell suddenly felt guilty for kissing Gertrude goodnight. Mr. Oliver put an arm around Lowell and asked him cheerfully, "My boy, do you think you can support my daughter?"[31] That question shook the romance right out of Lowell's head.

His relationship with Gertrude slowed down to a friendship.

The United States Bureau of Mines reported the 1906 gold output of the Cripple Creek-Victor Mining District to be $13,976,727. A few million dollars short of what the Victor **Daily Record** reported.

Dr. Thomas rented office space in the City Bank Building, the Central Drug Building, and Boston Clothing Building (Emergency Hospital) at various times during his seventeen years in Victor. The tracks of the electric interurban tram are visible on Victor Avenue. The Victor Daily Record was located half a block south (to the right) of the Central Drug Company. Most of the buildings in this photograph are still standing today.   Colorado Historical Society.

Circa 1906-1907: The Victor Opera House on East Victor Avenue and the tenderloin of First Street. It was a lively area for a paper route. A lot of human drama took place in the red-light district. The area was part of Lowell's delivery route in 1903-04.　　　　　　　　　　　　　　　　　Pikes Peak Library District

Goldfield was the third largest town in the district. The people of Victor and Goldfield felt a certain kinship, especially in the rivalry for community leadership over Cripple Creek. Just south of Independence, Lowell took on a paper route in Goldfield to help feed and shelter his burro.　　　Cripple Creek District Museum

1907

The new year was celebrated with exuberance. When midnight arrived, the Granite Mine let its large whistle blow. A chain reaction followed. Dozens of other mine whistles echoed through the district. The whistles kept up their raucous noise for five minutes. Then a loud array of shooting firecrackers and revolvers took over. Cannon crackers joined in and for the next half hour it could have been the Fourth of July. Drinking and good cheer continued until dawn.

The stores were closed all of 1 January.

On New Year's Day, Jane Kennark performed in Clyde Fitch's production of **The Toast of the Town.** The original full scale show was presented in the Victor Opera House. Jane Kennark played the character of Betty Singleton, the reigning beauty of the theater in the time of King George III.

Forest F. Latimer was the new manager of the opera house. He was the son of Dr. Latimer, and lived with the family at 220 South Sixth Street. He had been the bookkeeper for the Cripple Creek Coal and Transportation Company. The position of Dr. Latimer's son in the theater was a convenience for the Thomases. They met many of the actors and actresses backstage.

An excellent discovery was made in the Findley Mine. On the tenth level, at a depth of eight hundred and fifty feet, a twenty-seven foot wide ore shoot was revealed. The territory of the Shurtloff Claim, in which the strike was found, had been left unexplored by the Findley Consolidated Company for many years. Sylvanite ore was shipped at between $50 and $60 carload lots.

Components of the district were changing. A.E. Carlton had taken on the management of the drilling of the Roosevelt Deep Drainage Tunnel. This move increased his power in the mining camp and helped steady gold production. John T. Milliken and David H. Moffat combined their resources in hopes of eliminating Carlton's holdings. Carlton enlisted Spencer Penrose, Charles Tutt, Charles MacNeill, and other wealthy mine and mill owners on his side. The impending battle was to be decisive.

Most of the producing mines had gone beyond the depth of one thousand feet. Vast quantities of subterranean water flows were a major hindrance. In the early years of the district, this problem had been vanquished either through the use of pumps or drainage tunnels. An extremely deep and long drainage tunnel was a key factor in controlling the future of the entire camp.

Other factors were hindering the mining. The problem of carbonic acid gas in the mines of Bull Hill, Battle Mountain, and Raven Hill was a constant threat. New air filtration systems were needed. But their costs were expensive, and renovations extensive.

Stock manipulations and "salting" accusations continued to plague Stratton's Independence, Limited. John Hays Hammond would not relent with his detrimental allegations against the Cripple Creek-Victor Mining District. His ravings frightened away many foreign investors. Similar mining frauds left local investors penniless. Working capitol flowed to other mining districts.

Dr. Thomas was aware of these alterations in the district's prospects. The direction the changes were taking Victor did not appeal to him. He felt the need to look for new horizons.

The May Clothing Company, 311 Victor Avenue, had a fire sale. Ladies tailored suits were advertised for $10. Young men's suits were $4.95 to $6.45. Derby-ribbed men's underwear cost 39¢, stiff-bosom shirts 49¢. Coats and vests were $2.95 to $11.45, men's dress shoes $1.95 to $2.35. Men's high cut shoes sold for $3.45 to $4.45, and boys' school shoes $1.19.

The Fortune Club was running special prices on liquor. Mr. Harry Lang, proprietor, offered a gallon of ten year old whiskey for four dollars; eight year old, $3.25; and, six year old, $2.75. Most of Mr. Lang's California port, sherry, and claret were going for $1.45 a gallon. The Fortune Club delivered its goods to the customer's door by calling Victor 165 on the telephone.

A show Dr. and Mrs. Thomas would not have missed came to the Victor Opera House on 28 January. America's leading tragedian, John Griffith, appeared in the elaborate production of Shakespeare's **King Richard III**. Special fireproof scenery was used because of the innovational electrical effects. The superb costuming was only surpassed by the play's talented company of actors and actresses.

30 January: fire consumed the Economic Extraction Mill. It was the largest mill of its kind, built in Eclipse Gulch by the Woods Investment Company in 1899 for $532,000. The fire began at five in the morning in the main mill. Spreading rapidly, it destroyed the ore houses, assay office, and general offices. Smoke could be seen rising over the summit of Squaw Mountain from any standpoint in Victor. Then wind blew the thick smoke into the United Mines Transportation Tunnel. The smoke rose up the Gold Coin shaft and filtered into Victor.

Since the mill was not in use, insurance on the structures had not been kept up. Negotiations had been underway to convert the mill into a cyanide plant for processing gold ore. The mill was never rebuilt.

6 February, "Victor High School Notes" by Donald Kennedy: "A party of geologists went to the caves Saturday to examine the caves and also for an outing. They returned late Saturday evening very tired and footsore. Those who enjoyed the trip were Will Hayes, Ray Shaw, John Pascoe, Lowell Thomas, Mart Watson and Donald Kennedy, Vin Ruse, John

Curnow."* These were the same caves Lowell and his cousin Carl played in some years back. The hiking tours with his father, learning geology and botany, gave Lowell a definite advantage over his school buddies.

6 February: those residing on South Sixth Street were shocked to hear the news of a suicide in their area. Mrs. Neff had been tending to her daughter's sickness. The doctor's report stated that Mrs. Babbock--Mrs. Neff's daughter--was fatally ill. Mrs. Neff could not accept this. She told her son-in-law that she would kill herself if her daughter died.

Mrs. Babbock had been suffering from blood poisoning for a week. At 2:20 A.M., her illness took her.

8:30 A.M., Mrs. Neff walked into the Victor Hardware Company and paid $14.75 for a 38-calibre, double-action Colt revolver and fifty shells.

Late in the afternoon of the 6th, Viola Nordquist and Genevieve Brubaker, two young school girls, were playing near the vacant house at 317 South Sixth Street. When they opened the coal closet under the back stairway, they saw a woman who appeared to be too drunk to move or speak. The girls ran off and found two boys, Arthur Fox and Allan Dray. The boys looked at the woman and realized she had been shot. They took off to find Marshal Naylor.

At the scene, the marshal determined that Mrs. Neff placed the revolver next to her right temple while sitting upright in the coal closet. When she pulled the trigger, the bullet passed through her head, exiting the other side. The bullet then bent a board on the coal closet's wall. Her head fell forward, but the cold weather prevented her body from losing its sitting position.

The residence Mrs. Neff killed herself in had a reputation for being haunted. The house was only a block away from the Thomas home.

1 March was a special day at the high school. A male quartet consisting of Donald Kennedy, Ray Shaw, Joe Brill, and Homer Huffaker and a male sextet consisting of Lowell Thomas, Harry Black, Orrin Devy, George Toby, Walter Schoen, and Leonard Hart performed a number of selections before the school assembly.

That evening, "Emma Gertrude and George Toby gave a charming party for the high school set at their home...High five was the leading feature of entertainment, followed by a choice supper. The senior class colors, blue and white, were in evidence in the decorations."* The party was given to honor the day's events at the school. Lowell was among the thirty-three guests.

Lowell was a storehouse of surprises and ideas. He never lost those qualities. Being active as a youth set the pattern for the rest of his life. In 1919, he started his "With Allenby in Palestine and Lawrence in Arabia" show. He did not rest for the next two years. The show reached four million people in America, England, Scotland, Ireland, Australia, New Zealand, and Southern Asia.

There were days when he had to step back from his growing worldwide popularity and take account of how far his energy and voice had taken him in such a short time. In London's Covent Garden, he looked "out from the wings into the resplendent opera house, all red plush and glittering crystal" and "was suddenly conscious of how recently he had come down from our Colorado mountains."[32] He "mined" his motivating forces cautiously, similar to the way Winfield Stratton had "banked" on his Independence Mine.

Jack Dempsey had been injured in a mining accident in the Portland. He was treated by Dr. Elliott. The Red Cross Hospital, which had once been the Gold Coin Club on Diamond Avenue between Fourth and Fifth streets, had twenty-one beds, an operating room, steam-heat throughout, and baths. Some of its modern equipment included x-ray and Finsen-Ray machines. Dempsey remained in the hospital only a few days. He was released on 4 March.

The total gold production to-date for the district, according to the **Record's** 16 March anniversary issue, was $222,000,000. The Klondike region's production was now far behind. The Cripple Creek-Victor District was off to pursue the $300,000,000 mark of Kolar, India.

Gertrude Lamb, Hazel Moore, Edna Neuman, Lucille McAvoy, Ruth Emens, and Gladys Retallack formed a mysterious club. The boys in the school were agog with wonder. The girls met at Gladys Retallack's house at 318 South Fourth Street. This was just two blocks away from Lowell's home. Leonard Hart, Donald Kennedy, Joe Brill, John Pascoe, and Jay Herold would meet at Lowell's. They would come up with a strategy, then march over to Gladys' while the girls were meeting. All attempts to discover what this secret club was about were thwarted. The boys did find out, however, that the club's initials were "V.G." It was unclear whether the mystery or the girls kept the boys most interested.

Lowell turned fifteen on 6 April. He had grown rapidly, both mind and body, in Victor. His parents had helped quicken his pace. Happenings in Victor added their significance. At the turn of the century, Victor, Colorado, was one of the most important and newsworthy spots in the country. He was aware that "Victor was where the miners lived, and Victor was where the gold came from."[33] All of his life he was proud to say he lived in a mining town. He was saddened to learn his father was making preparations for the family to leave.

Charles B. Hanford and Miss Marie Drofnah appeared in **Julius Caesar** on 4 May at the Victor Opera House. Forty players were in the special company. The different settings for the play were of a grand scale: the great square in Rome, the Roman senate, conspiracy in Brutus' garden, quarrel scene in Brutus' tent, and the plains of Philippi were all presented in detail. The people of Victor could not get enough of Shakespeare.

The play was "An event of unusual artistic importance."* But it was Shakespeare's gift of words which enamored the people. Since Lowell had arrived in Victor, he had become increasingly cognizant of the power of words. A celebration or a riot could be caused by a few well-spoken lines in this vibrant mining town.

Alfred Patek brought his one-man show to Victor on 10 May. Patek's performance at the opera house had a profound effect upon Lowell. Patek was a traveler. He had a fine reputation as a journalist and a speaker. He had once been the editor of the Denver **Times**. The presentation concerned itself with Patek's recent trip to the Isthmus of Panama.

He gave an interesting talk about the Panama Canal, making his show entertaining as well as educational by telling his story through a human interest point-of-view. This type of show appealed to Lowell's adventurous spirit. The fifteen moving pictures and two hundred stereopticon lantern slides added to the highlights. Scenes from every day life to the landscape of the country made the show a living representation of Panama.

1915-16: Lowell incorporated portions of Patek's presentation methods into a new kind of "multi-media" production. His shows on Alaska were small-scale, but they received positive responses. He had brought along an Ernemann movie camera on his second trip into Alaska. He photograhed Fairbanks, a dangerous ride over snow-covered Valdez Trail in a Model T Ford, the Yukon River, the towns of St. Michael and Nome, and the salmon run at Cordova. Lowell added his first-hand adventures and witty monologue to his presentations.

The jump from the Alaska shows to the elaborate Allenby-Lawrence productions covered a vast expanse. Lowell, Fran (Lowell's first wife), and cameraman Harry Chase had over 100,000 feet of war scenes from France, Italy, the Middle East, and Germany to edit in 1919. After weeks of preparation, few people were interested in promoting a show on World War I. America had returned to pacifism.

Chase contacted Frank Robison of the New York **Globe**. Robison, who had done travelogues for newspapers in the past, talked the editor of the **Globe,** Fred B. Taintor, into fronting Lowell's show. Taintor thought he could boost the paper's circulation with the concept. Lowell had different ideas.

The Century Theater was booked. Window displays in Lord and Taylor's on Fifth Avenue in New York attracted large crowds. Spiked helmets from Wilhelm's army, Emir Feisal's Hejaz flag, the German flag, and placards announcing, "Direct from Jerusalem, Berlin and Paris! Lowell Thomas! Three Weeks Only!" were placed on exhibit. The Century was sold out the first night.

The show began with Levantine music chosen by Fran Thomas. The theater was dark. Lowell dramatically appeared in a spotlight. He opened with, "Come with me to lands of history, mystery and romance. What you are to see is an untold story, part of it as old as time, and part history in the making."[34] He stepped out of the main focus. A large screen surprised the audience with an exhilarating film panorama shot from the air. Lowell continued to narrate the mixture of various medias.

The show was very popular during its three-week engagement at the Century. The Allenby and Lawrence campaigns became the central focus. A larger theater was needed to accommodate the crowds. Madison Square Garden was booked.

Percy Burton, the famous British manager of such stars as Sarah Bernhardt, saw the show on its last night at the Garden. Backstage, Burton told Lowell he wanted to arrange an English engagement immediately. Lowell had already invested $20,000 in an American tour. So he told Burton that if he could play Covent Garden Royal Opera House and receive an invitation to perform for King George V, he would consider postponing the American shows. Burton came through. Lowell, Fran, and Harry were off to London.

The show was reworked for the English audiences. Rewriting and reediting filled the whole six week ocean journey. The show was retitled, "The Last Crusade--With Allenby in Palestine and Lawrence in Arabia". A Nile setting opened the production. An Oriental dance of seven veils was performed amidst faintly illuminated pyramids. Oriental music and a Mohammedan call to prayer guided the dancer's steps.

The first show in London was given a ten minute ovation.

The **Times, Morning Post,** and **Daily Telegraph** gave Lowell Thomas and his show grand reviews. Lines formed on all four sides of the opera building for tickets. Among the luminaries who saw the show were: Rudyard Kipling, George Bernard Shaw, Prime Minister David Lloyd George, Winston Churchill, Emir Feisal, General Allenby and his wife, Premier of France Georges Clemenceau, and T.E. Lawrence. The English could not get enough of Lowell's two-hour show.

Lord Burnham said of Lowell and his presentation at a banquet in the Criterion Restaurant atop Piccadilly Circus: "a great artist, a ripe scholar, a brave man...Lowell Thomas had almost created a new art."[35]

Exactly how strongly Alfred Patek's Panama show at the Victor Opera House in 1907 influenced Lowell would be nebulous to speculate. The ingredients of Patek's presentation were definitely improved upon by Lowell's innovational uses of medias. But the key factor which made the Allenby-Lawrence show so popular was its narrator--Lowell Thomas. His enthusiasm, oratorical abilities, eye for the human interest story, and sense of adventure made the presentation larger than life. The show itself was merely a vehicle in which Lowell Thomas' charismatic personality was placed on display.

Dr. Thomas was correct about the district being in a decline. The population of Victor had fallen to eight thousand. Production for the district, according to the U.S. Bureau of Mines, was $10,404,360. As the summer of 1907 drifted in, the Thomases moved to Greenville, Ohio.

1908

Victor, Colorado must have been incomparable in Dr. Thomas' eyes. The family was again residing in the City of Mines late in the summer of 1908. Their residence was a roomy two-story house at 317 North Fourth Street. Dr. Thomas had not found another town suitable to set up his practice.

Lowell had had an interesting school year in Ohio. He had qualified for the football team. His popularity had been of a mixed sort because of his Colorado mountain background. But his reputation changed when he easily won first place in an oratory contest. His entertaining delivery of Wendell Phillips' tribute to Toussaint L'Ouverture before the class assembly left no room for a second place. He was elected captain of the football team, and became known as "Two-gun" Lowell.

Back in Victor, Lowell was not about to take his speaking and performing talents for granted. Victor had changed, and so had Lowell. Confidence in himself made him excel to new heights. It would be less than a decade when the name of Lowell Thomas would surpass the fame of Victor.

Dr. Thomas rented Room 6 in the Postoffice Building, on the northeast corner of Third Street and Victor Avenue, for his medical office. He could be reached at work by calling Victor 302. The opera house was only one block east. B.P. Schoen's Pharmacy could easily be walked to by Dr. Thomas' patients. The Victor High School was in view a couple blocks east on Victor Avenue.

George Kyner still owned the **Record.** But he wanted to branch out his operation. He acquired the financial backing necessary to buy the Cripple Creek **Times.** The Kyners moved to Cripple Creek. John H. White became the managing editor of the **Record.** Rates dropped to fifty cents a month, and to five dollars a year.

Early in September, a mystic figure came to Victor. Dr. Alexander J. McIvor-Tyndall, leader of the New Thought Movement and editor of **Swastika Magazine,** was promoting his new organization. Tyndall claimed he was a "student of the psychology of life." He was purported to have been gifted with psychic and clairvoyant powers. Tyndall must have had some kind of talent because he kept the people of Victor mystified with his talks and psychic demonstrations for nearly two weeks.

6 September: Dr. McIvor-Tyndall held his first series of lectures at Elks Hall. "The Coming Man and His Marvelous Developments" set the mood for his brand of thought. Displays of "startling and mysterious manifestations of occult powers, including thought transference, telepathy, psychometry, clairvoyance and odic forces"* followed each of Tyndall's lectures.

He rented Suite 207 of the Bank Building on the northeast corner of Fourth and Victor Avenue. He offered his clairvoyant skills during the hours of 9 A.M. to 1 P.M., 2 P.M. to 4 P.M., and 7 P.M. to 9 P.M. Readings were one, two, and five dollars. Seats at his lectures were fifty cents. During his ten day visit, Tyndall spoke on "Fate", "How Thought Can Kill", "Ghosts", "Every Man A King", and "Personal Magnetism."

During the Labor Day Celebration, a mysterious lady of fashion disembarked in Victor from the daily train. Her appearance caused a lot of talk. She was dressed in the latest fashion from the East Coast--a "Directorie" gown. The dress exposed a good portion of dark silk stocking up to the woman's knees. Light blue garters with pearl settings were also in view. Her alluring stride was supported by three inch heel "slippers." She walked about Victor Avenue for awhile, looking in the store windows. Then she boarded the next train to Colorado Springs. The woman's name was never learned, but her fashionable appearance became an annual event in Victor for some years.

31 October: "The Sigma Gamma fraternity of the Victor High School gave a delightful Halloween party at the Schoen home Saturday evening. The house was beautifully decorated in pumpkin vines and jack-o-lanterns furnished the light. The fireplace was the center of attraction. The favored guests were Miss Electa Franklin, Miss Edna Neuman, Miss Helen Jones, Miss Gertrude Oatman, Miss Margaret McClanahan, Miss Ruth Emens, Jack Pascoe, Homer Huffaker, Jay Herold, Allen Dray, Clyde Eddy, Will Haynes, Lowell Thomas, Leslie Schoen and Walter Schoen."*

Jay Herold quit school before his graduation. He had decided to pursue other prospects. Lowell was concerned over his friend's sudden shift in plans. But Jay felt the opportunity to work at A.E. Carlton's City Bank in Victor was not one he should pass up. Lowell and the rest of the boys at the high school kept Jay involved in their activities.

1 December: "It is now certain that the students of the Victor High School will have a magazine. A magazine to be prepared by the students in every way with the exception of the printing."* The Cripple Creek High School already had a newspaper. Lowell, Donald Kennedy, Clyde Eddy, Forest Benedict, and others felt the Victor High School could also support such a publication.

The **Record** recommended: "At present time in the high schools and colleges, news matter of the school is paid more attention to than is the literary side. To make a bright paper, one that the students will be eager for, it is suggested that the news of the high school be given precedence to the stories." The human interest tale was the key to a paper's success. The **Record** was an excellent example of this philosophy.

By popular vote, the paper was named **The Sylvanite.** Lowell became managing editor. Financial backing was facilely arranged. By 2 December, the **Record** was happy to report that the "board of editors is doing all in its power to make the paper a success from a literary and news stand point." The first issue was ready for distribution by the second week of December.

In February 1909, the paper was enjoying a healthy circulation. Lowell J. Thomas '09 was listed as the senior editor. Forest Benedict '10 was junior editor. John Pascoe was alumni editor. Each issue cost ten cents; a year's subscription was seventy-five cents. Lowell's touch was everywhere.

In "Editorials": "Those of us who see mountains every day scarcely ever to stop to look at the real beauty of the magnificent scenery which we have around us; those who see its wonder only once in awhile stand to gaze with awe at the marvels...The lofty mountains covered with snow should be bold leaders constantly before us, telling us to set our aims and plans as high and pure as they themselves."

In human interest: "The class of 1909 is fairly well represented in athletics of Victor High School. There are three girls and two boys from this class on the basket ball teams."

"The senior class is very wise. No one had to take the history of Spanish examinations."

In humor: "When it is cold on high school hill Shakespeare becomes popular. A few mornings ago (John) Pascoe was heard to mutter--'Friends, Romans and countrymen, lend me your ears; mine are frozen."

And in thoughtfulness: "Do you know the importance of the Literary Society?...A literary society is practical and beneficial throughout. How many of us can rise and express our thoughts, clearly and in good English, without previous preparation. Very few, I am sure. There is work in the Victorian that develops just that ability in a man, and later on we may have reason to thank the 'powers that be' for the preparation we received in this line...The ability to debate a question clearly and forcibly is of the greatest value to all of us." Lowell was very prophetic in this section of **The Sylvanite,** at least where his own future was concerned.

1908 ended on an optimistic note. The Dante No. 2 Shaft hit a rich quartz vein on the three-hundred-foot level of the mine. The four-foot-wide vein was covered with a spongy material colored dull brown. The material assayed out at between 82.2 to 114 ounces of gold per ton, a monetary value of $1,644 to $2,280. Sacks of the ore were placed in a bank vault while awaiting shipment.

The 1908 output in gold was reported as $16,230,525 by the U.S. Bureau of Mines.

Garfield (right) was the elementary school Lowell attended when he first came to Victor. The third grade class was full so he became the youngest fourth grader in the school. At Victor High (left), in 1908-09, Lowell was senior editor of the school's newspaper--The Sylvanite.   Colorado Historical Society

The Victor High School Graduating Class of 1909. This was the school's thirteenth graduation. There were thirteen students in the class. Lowell Thomas is pictured second from the left in the top row.   Victor/Lowell Thomas Museum

1909

The year promised to be productive. Stratton's Independence, Limited opened a new mill on the first day of January. The mill site covered fifteen acres on the southeast side of Battle Mountain. It consisted largely of a crusher building, a mixing building, and a roasting building. One hundred tons of ore could be processed per day.

"Several young gentlemen of Victor have organized a social club and have very swell apartments in the Baltimore Hotel. The latest literature will be one of the attractions and athletics will be the principal entertainment. The officers are: W.H. Luhman, president; Jay Herold, treasurer; Andy George, secretary. Other members are: J.G. Pascoe, Frank Elliott, Dick Wilson, Parks Van Dolah, Claude Berlin, Lowell Thomas, Will Hayes, Joe Brill and Charles Eddy.''* The most popular sports among the "young gentlemen" were: football, boxing, track--all of which Lowell participated in. As for literature: Frank Norris, Mark Twain, Edgar Allan Poe, Sir Walter Raleigh, William Shakespeare, Goethe, Byron, Disraeli, and Rudyard Kipling were their immediate favorites.

Lowell was deeply influenced by a wide range of writers. Plato's transcriptions of Socrates' philosophy, Julius Caesar's military memoirs of the Gallic and civil wars, Boccaccio's **Decameron**, the autobiography of Cellini, the poetry of Sir Walter Raleigh, the plays of William Shakespeare, the axioms of Benjamin Franklin, Goethe's **Faust,** the romanticism of Lord Byron, the fiction of Alexander Dumas, Victor Hugo, and Benjamin Disraeli, and the incomparable psycho-horrific short stories of Edgar Allan Poe. Contemporaries like Mark Twain, Frank Norris, Booth Tarkington, Thomas Hardy, George Bernard Shaw, Oscar Wilde, and Rudyard Kipling were also intricate in helping Lowell to form his own writing style.

Early in 1909, Victor started on a "Western" trend. After 1899, when Stratton sold his Independence Mine to the Venture Corporation, British influence had been strong in the district. Now, European fashion was fading in Victor. The "Old West" had always existed beneath the cosmopolitan facade. With the disappearance of foreign investment, the town resumed its true form.

F.F. Latimer brought in the American cowboy play, **In Wyoming.** It was staged at the opera house on 31 January. The play touted Miss Dunsmore as the beautiful leading lady. Latimer advertised the show as "a genuine western comedy void of the usual gun play." The production was so popular that Latimer arranged to have Owen Wister's **The Virginian** at the opera house on 5 February. W.S. Hart played the Virginian and Frank Champeau was Trampas.

5 February: a sizeable earthquake shook the district. Windows rattled and china clanked together in cabinets, but no heavy damage or loss of life was reported. Rumor blamed the massive workings in the mines for the quake.

13 February: "The Frat Club of the Victor High School (Sigma Gamma) will enjoy a very pleasant party this evening at the home of Allan Dray on South Seventh Street. Games and music and a dainty luncheon will add to the evening's pleasure...."* Although Lowell was a guest at this party, his time for social affairs was lessening. He was busy preparing himself for college. His father tutored him in subjects the public school did not offer. And, he brushed up on subjects in which he was weak. To finance a portion of his higher education, he worked as an assay rider for the Portland Mine.

There were times, however, when he found time to be mischievous. Armory Hall sponsored dances on Saturday nights. The Port Wine Club scheduled a dance and all of Lowell's buddies wanted to attend. They were already drinking rum by the time Lowell joined them. Lowell drank root beer. If the boys had brought vodka, he might have had a few shots.

When they arrived at the dance, it looked as if the tenderloin had moved its parlours into the hall. Smoke clouded the air and the smell of liquor stung the nostrils. Lowell caught sight of a girl seductively attired in a tight black dress. His friends were more intent upon drinking than dancing. But he was infatuated with the girl. Two hours passed before he asked her to dance.

Waltzing around the floor, he employed his finest words to tell the young lady about his wild exploits about town. His stories were tall, bordering on pure fiction. The young woman liked dancing with him. They continued on past midnight. He was in the middle of one of his best tales when he suddenly felt the stare of his father. Lowell turned towards the main entrance. His father was standing in the doorway. A look of deep concern was etched upon Dr. Thomas' face.

Lowell had no choice. He left the girl in the center of the dance floor and walked sheepishly to his father. The walk back to the house was a silent march. Once inside, Lowell was given a two-hour lecture on the sordid happenings of the tenderloin. Dr. Thomas told him about some of the pathetic cases he had treated in the red-light district when he was city physician. His message became explicitly clear to Lowell.

Lowell was a member of the Senior Class Committee for the 1909 graduates. The others on the committee were Anna Bullock, Gertrude Lamb (Oliver), Homer Huffaker, and Edna Neuman. They decided to start celebrating early in the year.

"The graduating Class, VHS '09, gave a very delightful party on Friday evening at the home of Miss Gertrude and Frances Lamb complimentary to the faculty of the high school. The parlor was decorated in the class colors of red and white. Blue and white added to the beauty of the dining room and library was beautiful in an artistic arrangement of yellow and white. It was undecided who received the lemon...."* Lowell attended this gathering of twenty-two people on 12 March. His math teacher, Mr. Lady, was present. Some interesting words must have passed between teacher and student.

The Victor High School had been remodeled in 1909. Special classrooms were incorporated in the school building. Modern physics and chemistry laboratories were installed. "Nature-study" materials like geological specimen cabinets became pertinent teaching tools. A modern gymnasium and auditorium were also added.

3 April: "Miss Edna Neuman entertained informally but very pleasantly at cards on Tuesday evening. Miss Electa Franklin, Gertrude Lamb, Lowell Thomas, Parks Van Dolah, and Leslie Schoen were present."*

The Victor Opera House continued to court its love for Shakespeare. **Othello** was staged on 17 April and **The Winter's Tale** followed on 18 April. A cast of thirty, with Charles B. Hanford and Miss Marie Drofnah as the leads, presented the plays. Lowell attended the showing of **The Winter's Tale** with John Pascoe and some other friends. They wanted to compare their past amateur production with one that was professional.

18 April was a long night in Victor. At 4:20 A.M., a house at 105 North First Street was dynamited. Two sticks of giant powder were used, but only one hundred dollars' worth of damage was done. The two women living in the house, Lillie Powers and Clara Henry, were thrown several feet out of their beds. Neither was injured. A few minutes after the blast, North First Street was filled with a curious array of barely clad people.

Senior graduation was nearing. Something extraordinary had to be planned. Plays were often given by the graduating class, but the 1909 seniors wanted to do something different. There were only thirteen people in the class, so options were limited. A senior ball of luxuriant style was decided upon.

8 May: "The senior ball to be given by the class of '09 of the Victor High School will be quite the event of the coming week. The class colors of red and white will artistically decorate the hall and nothing will be left undone to make this the event of the season...."*

Lowell was part of the "crowd from the Senior class of Victor High School '09 which met with Miss Gertrude Lamb Wednesday evening and perfected arrangements for the Senior Ball to be given at Armory Hall on Thursday evening May 13th."* The ball was the first of its kind to be sponsored by a graduating class. It was called the First Annual Dance and Promenade. Over seventy-five guests attended. There was music, refreshments, and elegant decorations.

12 May: "Lowell Thomas was most delightfully and completely surprised on Wednesday evening when the senior class of Victor High School of which he is a popular member gathered at his home at 317 North Fourth Street and enjoyed a delightful evening in various games, music and dainty

luncheon."* Since his seventeenth birthday had already passed, the most probable reason for this celebration was his acceptance to the University of Northern Indiana in Valparaiso.

27 May: the graduation ceremony of the Senior Class of 1909 was held at the Victor Opera House. It began at 8 P.M. The commencement was the thirteenth for the high school. Thirteen students graduated: Ruth A. Emens, Gertrude Viola Lamb, Stephonia Potochnick, Edna Neuman, Electa Franklin, Anna Mae Bullock, Emeline Jones, William Elmer Dodsworth, Harold Sidney Worcester, Nash Glau, Lowell Jackson Thomas, Frances Joseph Needham, and William P. Hayes.

All of the students gave a speech, performed a song, or took some special part in the program. The diplomas were handed out by the president of the school board, George E. Simonton. The benediction was given by Reverend Father Edward Downey. The stage was decorated to represent a woodland scene. Potted ferns and palms were placed just behind the footlights; geraniums with red blooms were located at regular intervals. The red and white class pennant was hung at the back of the stage. The girls wore white dresses and the boys dark suits.

The program was lengthy but diversified. The presentations were smooth and entertaining. Lowell Jackson Thomas gave the commencement address:

"William Howard Taft.

"On the world's stage, events of momentous importance, periods of lasting effect, are constantly being drawn out and impressed upon the pages of history. We look back upon those actors whose names are immortal and regard them with an awe and reverence due none but the divine while men of equal caliber are playing their roles before our very eyes.

"We are now entering upon the period of a new administration and the eyes of all the nation are turned upon him, who shall for the next four years carry out the desires of the people who have bestowed upon him the highest honor which it is in their power to give. On September 15, 1857 at Cincinnati, in the state of Ohio, which had already acquired the title of president producer, a man was born, destined to emphasize still further Ohio's right to that name. William Howard Taft made his entrance into this world the son of a rich man. His father Alphonso Taft was an American statesman and jurist of high rank, occupying at different times such offices as: Minister to Russia, Judge of the supreme court of Cincinnati and attorney general of the United States.

"Young Taft, while at college, held the honor of being the largest man who had entered Yale up to that time but not withstanding avoirdupois to the amount of three hundred pounds, he made a remarkable record as a stu-

84

dent and leader, never before in the history of that famous institution were prizes and scholarships monopolized as by him. Important school affairs were brought to Taft for decision for the unusual deliberation and sense which have marked his later career were also characteristic of him as a collegian.

"Henry Cabot Lodge says: 'Successful men are those who take advantage of their opportunities for opportunities are not made by men but for them.' It would almost seem that Taft is an exception to this rule, for in the words of George Fitch, 'early in life opportunity coming to knock at the Taft door found that gentleman had already gone out and gotten a job.' After graduating from Yale, he returned to Cincinnati, and became a newspaper reporter, a field of work which could not but broaden his education. Next he entered politics and became prominent as a prosecuting attorney of Hamilton county, revenue collector, judge of the supreme court of Cincinnati, solicitor general of the United States and a little later Dean of the Cincinnati Law school.

"President McKinley, recognizing Taft's remarkable capacity for work, appointed him at the head of the commission for organizing a civil government in the Phillippines and he was made governor in 1901. We now enter upon the most remarkable period of work thus far in his career, out of the fertile mind of Taft issued the governmental designs for our newly acquired possessions. The responsibility placed upon his shoulders was enormous, particularly as the eyes of the whole critical world were watching to see what more we could do for the uncivilized Filipinos than had been done by their former tyrannical masters.

"While chief executive of our insular possessions, Taft established civil government in all the provinces, provided for public education of the most advanced character, and implanted judiciary, health, postal, and civil service systems such remarkable administration is rarely met with.

"At the beginning of Roosevelt's first administration, Taft was called home to fill an office in the cabinet. As secretary of war, he conducted the affairs of his department with a broad, courageous, and skillful statesmanship that has won the admiration of the world. As a party leader and presidential candidate, he enjoyed such loyal and enthusiastic support as is scarcely to be paralleled in history. His highest ambition has been to be a judge of the supreme court of the United States, but resigning himself to the desire of the people he, accepted the presidential nomination July 1908.

"Did ever a man receive better preparation for the occupancy of our highest office? Charles H. Clark in the Independent says of Mr. Taft: 'He is as strong as he is gentle. His reputation is simply spotless. In all the aggitation of a heated campaign for the greatest office of the world no one has ventured to intimate a doubt of the absolute honesty of this man who has been before the country for a quarter of a century. Nor can anyone successfully dispute the simple proposition that in the whole history of the United States no one ever named for the presidency who has so fitted by nature, by training and by experience for the duties, dignities and responsibilities of that unique office.'

"Just preceding Taft's nomination, Theodore Roosevelt said of him: 'I think Mr. Taft is the strongest candidate before the convention, we need just his qualities in the coming campaign.'

"He is clean, forceful, courageous, a man who will not hesitate to stand by his convictions whether that be popular or not.

"And a man of brilliant mind, of broad views and of sturdy inflexible integrity such a leader the country needs today to carry on the government of the people. That is of indomitable courage and of energetic patriotism. Of all the brilliant statesmen in our American political history there is no abler man, no sounder man, no better fighter, no man who honors the state and nation more or has rendered them better service than our present president, William Howard Taft."

(This speech was printed in the Victor **Daily Record** on 28 May 1909. No other printing has been found. The editorial mistakes were those of the **Record's,** not Mr. Thomas'. It is evident from this address, written at the age of seventeen, why Mr. Thomas, at the age of 88, gave Mr. Reagan's seconding speech at the 1980 Republican Convention. Mr. Thomas' seventy-one years of practice at writing speeches made his style an event.)

At the end of the graduation ceremony, cut flowers were placed upon the stage in great quantities. Ruth Emens, president of the class, presented a gold-handled umbrella from the senior class to W.S. Roe, principal of the school.

Throughout his life, Lowell stayed in contact with all of the people with whom he graduated. In August 1981, he picked up a picture of his graduating class in the Lowell Thomas Exhibit of the Victor/Lowell Thomas Museum. He named every person in the picture, related stories about them, and told of each individual's achievements.

Bob Womack, the discoverer of the Cripple Creek-Victor Mining District, died 10 August 1909 in a house at 117 South Limit Street in Colorado Springs. The time was 6:30 A.M. Womack was penniless. He was buried in the same cemetery as Winfield Scott Stratton. Stratton had been one of the few who had helped Womack during his bouts with poverty. Finally, Bob rested in richer ground.

$11,499,093 was the gold output for the district in 1909.

Circa 1916-17: Dr. Thomas and daughter, Pherbia, standing in front of Victor house on 227 South Sixth Street. The Thomas family was about to leave the district to make their new home in New Jersey.

Victor Avenue, looking west.

Hardrock mining was difficult and costly. Man and machine endured tests of strength every minute work was performed in the mines. The equipment was built for breaking through extremely solid rock--granite. The men, a courageous lot with unlimited stamina, suffered the greatest of hardships: they were surrounded by rock walls hundreds of feet beneath the surface of the earth with a myriad of dangers ready to drop on them at any moment.

Attire for the miner varied. Metal helmets were rare. Felt hats were more common. Candles were often their main sources of light until electric cables could be strung into the deep drifts they worked in. The shaft house of the Gold Coin possessed stained glass windows, comfortable changing rooms, pool tables, and a library. The shaft house of the Mary McKinney was not so elegant.

1911-1912

The mysterious lady of fashion arrived once more in Victor on 4 July 1911. She had been in the City of Mines in 1910. A "harem" dress had been displayed to all passing her on Victor Avenue. In 1911, the "octagonal" skirt was in style in the East.

The train pulled into the station at 1:30 P.M. Chief of Police Nolan was at the depot, waiting in expectation. The fashionable lady stepped out of her car. All eyes were upon her. The eight-sided skirt, yellow and trimmed in green, was much more exquisite than the recent "pants" designs. She attracted so much attention that she asked for police protection. Nolan was more than pleased to offer his assistance.

After walking up and down Victor Avenue, she departed on the Colorado Springs train at 3:30 P.M. Already the men were wondering what next year's fashion would be.

Later in July, the first motorized vehicle used in the mines appeared in Victor. The five-ton Pierce-Arrow truck was brought up to the district on 28 July. On the 29th, the truck was given its first test. It moved one thousand six hundred pounds of ore from the Portland Mine in an hour's time. A double set of wheels had been placed on the rear axle of the vehicle so it could climb steep grades. The success of the truck marked the beginning of the end of animal labor in the district.

30 July: Cooney Miller and Fritz Kahe, described as "two hopheads",* were thrown in jail for vagrancy. They had left Victor earlier in the day but their need for cocaine turned them around in their tracks. The police had no idea what to do with them. If the "two hopheads" did not constantly have "coke in their veins" they were "half crazy" and made "everyone with whom they came in contact feel nearly the same way."*

2 August: the city of Victor started issuing automobile licenses. Owners of autos had demanded it. They had been experiencing trouble while "motoring" in other cities. If an automobile did not have a license, the owner was forced to buy one in each town he drove through. The city council of Victor acted. Licenses were issued for three dollars a year. Walter Stevens of the Antlers Cafe was lucky enough to receive the "No. 1" plate. Licenses were such a boon to the city treasury that every year the council raised their prices.

Sunday, 13 August: a pleasant rain fell over Victor. 9:15 in the evening, the rain stopped. A full moon filled the fresh night air. Suddenly a rainbow appeared. The entire color spectrum was represented. It shone brilliantly for five minutes before a second rainbow came into view. The night sky was radiating with color. The natural light show lasted for thirty minutes.

In 1910, gold production had been $15,878,000. Both the Portland and Independence mills were using new processes which allowed profit from ore which contained as little as three-twentieths of an ounce per ton.

In the beginning of 1911, the Roosevelt Deep Drainage Tunnel had been completed. Water flow averaged six thousand gallons per minute. New depths could be reached in the mines. Years were added to the life of the district.

With all the improvements in mining operations, 1911 looked to be a productive year. The grand total for the district was sure to surpass three hundred million dollars.

Improvements in the town were seen. The Baltimore Hotel on North Third Street was remodeled. It was now the largest in Victor. It was three stories high and had fifty large rooms for rent. The Baltimore's management decorated their establishment with comfortable, home-like furniture. There was a dining hall for guests, a special commercial dining room, and the German Beer Hall.

Charles Bosick and John Bindschaedler ran the German Beer Hall. It was located on the first floor of the hotel. The menu was long and exotic. There were domestic and Key West cigars. Imported wines like Niersteiner for $1.50 a bottle. Cheeses from all over the world. Lord Kitchner Sardines from Norway cost twenty cents a plate. Prime Russian Caviar was forty cents a serving. Old Taylor, Old Crow, and Canadian Club--all whiskies--sold for fifteen cents a drink. Three Star Hennessy Brandy cost twenty-five cents for two drinks. Coors, Hof Brau, Schlitz Special Brew, Budweiser, Blue Ribbon, Spaten Brau, Bass Ale, and Guiness Stout were between fifteen and thirty-five cents a bottle. The German Beer Hall catered to professional men. Its owners felt the "dingy barroom was a thing of the past."*

Lowell Thomas had been seventeen when he left Victor to attend college in Indiana. His parents had moved to a home at 227 South Sixth Street in 1910. When Lowell returned to Victor near the end of August 1911, Pherbia was seven years old, his father still had an office in the Postoffice Building, and his mother was still actively participating in church functions. He had earned two degrees at college: Bachelor of Science and Master of Arts.

Ralph Carr--later, governor of Colorado--was editor of the Cripple Creek **Times** in August 1911. He had this to say about Lowell's homecoming:

> "Another Victor boy has returned home with honors earned in literary lines at higher institutions of learning. Lowell Thomas, son of Dr. H.G. Thomas and a graduate of the Victor High School, arrived in the city yesterday (28 August 1911) from Valparaiso, Ind., where he secured a Bachelor of Arts degree last week.
>
> "Young Thomas, who was well known because of his scholarship and athletic ability, graduated from the

Victor High School in the class of 1909 and immediately entered the University of Valparaiso where he has been attending school ever since. He has returned to spend the next few months in this city (Victor) and will probably enter the law department of the University of California in January.

"Thomas made a good record at the Indiana institution."

A "good record" was an understatement. Lowell had obtained two degrees in two years. From all Dr. Thomas' teachings, Lowell had narrowed his choice of careers to one field: law. In 1907, he had witnessed a trepanning operation performed by his father. After the patient's skull had been opened and the brain exposed, he could not hold back his urge to regurgitate. At that point, it had become evident that the practice of medicine did not suit Lowell. Attending Valparaiso, he had pursued his goal vigorously, taking both freshman and sophomore classes in his first year, and both junior and senior classes in his second. At the age of nineteen, Lowell was prepared to enter law school.

Lowell refamiliarized himself with friends and places. Homer Huffaker had returned from farming in eastern Colorado. Ruth Emens was a teacher at Garfield School. Stephonia Potochnick was also a teacher at Garfield. Edna Neuman was a teacher at South Goldfield School. Electa Franklin was still living with her parents at 410 Lee Avenue. Emeline Jones was a teacher in the Cameron School.

William Dodsworth, Harold Worcester, Nash Glau, Frances Needham, and William Hayes had left Victor.

Jay Herold was a clerk in the Victor Hardware Supply Company. His father was the manager. Both lived at 509 Portland Avenue. The Victor Hardware Supply Company was located at 412 Victor Avenue, and owned by M.S. Rankin and Sam Rankin.

John Pascoe was an ore sorter at the Carnduff and Duncan Mine. His residence was a room in the Baltimore Hotel. Leslie Schoen had joined his father in the drugstore business at 110 North Third Street. Anna Bullock was a teacher at Garfield School.

Lowell and his friends were ready for the big Labor Day Celebration. The events for the spectacle were somewhat different from what they had been. Bronco busting was the main attraction. Many of the participants of Cheyenne, Wyoming's Frontier Days were in town.

"Bugger" Red, champion of wild horse riding, came to Victor in late August. Red was a fearless rider in this particular contest. He claimed his specialty was the "bad and wild ones".* The higher his horses jumped, the wider his smile opened. "Buffalo" Vernon, who rode steers and zebras, was also in town. Vernon liked taking pictures while riding his wild animals. Goldie St. Clair, champion of the lady bronco busters, arrived for the celebration with her husband, Bernie St. Clair. Jim Smith, A.L.

Clark, Hugh Clark, and Charles McKinley were all in Victor for "Top of the World Days."

The celebration took place on 4 and 5 September. There were three world championships and two western championships scheduled. A total of $5,000 in prizes was to be awarded the winners. It was billed as "Two days of the biggest fun ever indulged in by a Western mining camp."* All sorts of contests had been lined up: double- and single-hand drilling, hitchcutting, "Bronco" busting, businessman's smoker, steer riding, horse races, cowboy races, cowgirl races, relay races, and a volunteer hose race.

A new contest was introduced for this special event: wrestling on horseback. Riders approached each other on the barebacks of horses. Each rider would then try to get a secure hold on his opponent, hoping to unseat him. "Bugger" Red signed up for this contest as did Dr. C.E. Elliott, Fire Chief Flannagan, Jim Massey, Dr. R.R. Walker, and many others.

Marshal of the Day was Nelson Franklin. The parade started on East Victor Avenue and continued for one and a half miles. Ten thousand people attended. Fritz Krog, a New York magazine writer, covered the entire celebration. The City of Mines was the "Top of the World on the map."*

The "bronco" busting brought back memories for Lowell. In 1909, he rode assay for the Portland Mine. This entailed collecting samples of ore from the mines and taking them to assay offices for estimates of gold content. He recalled one day when the slow pace of his horse, the heat of the day, and the familiarity of the trail put him to sleep. He had not been aware of how long he had been dozing when a whistle of a train frightened his horse. Before he was fully reawakened, the horse was running at a furious charge. He lost his balance on the saddle. But he managed to regain control of the horse before he was tangled up on the horse's underside. It was not the last frightful adventure he was to have with a horse.

1949: Lowell and his son were on their way back from Lhasa, the "Forbidden City" of Tibet. They had exchanged their mules for untamed horses. For a day and a half, Lowell's previous riding experience had served him well. But he made one serious mistake. He had gotten off his mount to look at some minerals alongside the trail. After finding what he was looking for, he tried remounting his horse, forgetting that it was necessary to have someone hold the reins. The horse threw him over the side of the steep trail. He landed on a ledge of sharp rocks. His hip was broken in eight places.

No effective pain killers had been packed in their first aid kits. The elevation was some 17,000 feet above sea level. The air was thin and the weather cold. Lowell attributed the saving of his life to Lowell Thomas, Jr.'s ability to take efficient control of the situation and his own excellent health. Not only was his life saved, but in May 1950 he was skiing the Juneau Ice Cap of Alaska.

Even with two college degrees in 1911, Lowell had no choice but to work in the mines. "And so I did what young scholars in mining camps have always done: I took a job swinging a pick and shovel...."[36] He mucked in the Portland Mine. All those familiar aches and pains resulting from hard physical exertion came back to him.

Lowell was fortunate, though. Word reached George Kyner that he was in Victor. It so happened Kyner needed an editor for the Victor **Daily Record.** Kyner called Lowell. Before the conversation ended, Lowell was working as editor of the **Record** for ninety-five dollars a month. He quickly found out his job entailed being not only editor but "reporter...legman, rewrite man and front man for reader complaints."[37] He was almost the entire staff of the newspaper. But he was not disappointed. It was better than working in the mines.

Kyner had offered Lowell a start in journalism. The work was never-ending, but the opportunity was most timely. He made the best of his chance. He quickly learned the meaning and value of the human interest story. "In any given ten-day period, you could count on a shooting spree in a gambling hall or one of the red-light districts, a holdup, a fire, a mine accident and an indignant reader proposing to horsewhip the editor. There were also rodeos, prizefights, evangelists heralding imminent doom for sinners--duly reported also were fraternal-order marching competitions with the winner sometimes decided by a general brawl that extended the length of Victor Avenue and drew the biggest crowds of all. It was an opportunity to intrigue any young man with a taste for the great human drama, and at the time this just suited me."[38]

1 October: the Victor Opera House staged a play which Lowell reviewed for the paper. Eugene Prebury had dramatized Rex Beach's story of the last frontier, **The Barrier.** This play about Alaska was on its first transcontinental tour, boasting the complete New York cast from the New Amsterdam Theater. Norval MacGregor played the character of John Gale and Eleanor Haber played Necia. The scenic production was superb. It portrayed Alaska as the land of eternal snow.

The performance remained in Lowell's mind. Three years later he journeyed to Alaska to experience the adventures of the land for himself.

Early in 1912, Sam Rankin and a group of Denver businessmen asked Lowell to be the editor of their newspaper, the Victor **News.** The pay was one hundred and thirty-five dollars a month. He had been doing a commendable job on the **Record.** Circulation was improving. But Kyner's promise of a raise in salary and increase in staff had not materialized. Lowell accepted Rankin's offer and moved into the **News'** office at 110 1/2 South Fourth Street.

"I never regretted moving on, but the fact is that nothing much changed at first. Victor was still a boomtown and I was still covering all the action."[39] Sam Vidler was also hired to work on the Victor **News.** Lowell was often tempted to print stories he had about Vidler, but everyone knew that Mrs. Vidler was dangerously jealous. Vidler was the general manager. John White was in charge of circulation.

War was on between the **News** and the **Record** when Lowell switched jobs. He knew that circulation was boosted by "a daily dose of sex, sensationalism or, at the very least, the picture of a pretty girl on the front page."[40] The newspaper tactics of William Randolph Hearst were needed for this "no-holds-barred battle for readers."[41]

One day, Lowell had the headline "BLAZE SWEEPS LOCAL BUILDINGS!" set on a three-inch typeset on the front page to attract attention. Frank Arkens, once an editor of the **Record,** came into the **News** office and asked Lowell how many buildings had actually burned. Lowell told him only three. Arkens replied, "Well, I tell you what kid, I'd try to hold something back for the Second Coming."[42]

The quest for the most sensational human interest story was always bubbling in Lowell. It became engrained in his character. There were plenty of stories to chose from in Victor. But the search never ended as long as the sun came up the next day.

His first active year in newspaper reporting prepared him for a significant turning point in his life. In 1914, after two years of study at the University of Denver, he went to Chicago to pursue his law education. He was hired as a reporter for the **Chicago Evening Journal.** He also attended classes at the Chicago-Kent College of Law. The editor of the **Journal,** Dick Finnegan, put Lowell on a story concerning a man named Carlton Hudson. It did not take long for Lowell's intuition and ingenuity to discover the truth behind Hudson's "success".

Hudson had an uncommon amount of old people leave him large sums of money in their wills. He was considered a financier. Many wealthy older women had made Hudson their financial adviser. His own riches grew rapidly. Lowell interviewed Hudson. A few key details gave Lowell the clues he needed to research Hudson's background.

Hudson possessed an educated accent indicating an Eastern background. Lowell sent letters to many Eastern institutions hoping to gain a lead. He used a familiar Victor ploy: he claimed Hudson was heir to a paying gold mine and wanted to know where Hudson could be reached. A school in Vermont identified a Carlton Hudson Betts. In the New York **World's** files, Lowell located two full folders on Betts. As it came to light, the philanthropic Chicago financier was really a New York con man.

A warrant was outstanding for Betts' arrest. With his editor's permission, Lowell visited Charles S. Whitman, the Governor of New York. A deal was arranged. The **Chicago Evening Journal** was granted a twenty-four hour lead on the story. New York got Carlton Hudson Betts.

Lowell was on the front page with a story every young reporter dreamed about.

But his good fortune did not stop at the headlines, a raise in salary, and a bonus. Silas Strawn, the head of one of Chicago's most prestigious law firms, asked Lowell to see him. He easily found the time. Strawn congratulated him on his story, and then informed him that some of the largest meat packing houses in Chicago were in his debt. Betts had been blackmailing these companies with information he had uncovered concerning a Texas oil deal. By discovering the truth behind Carlton Hudson Betts, and thus leading to his arrest, Lowell had inadvertently rid the meat packing companies of a dangerous burden. Strawn told Lowell that if he ever needed anything, he should contact him without delay.

In 1917, Lowell was back in Strawn's office. His need: financial backing for Secretary Lane's project dealing with American news coverage of World War I. Eighteen millionaires, whom Strawn represented, and Strawn himself, raised $100,000 for Lowell's job as war correspondent. These grateful millionaires were unaware that they were helping send Lowell Thomas to one of the most important news stories of the twentieth century--Lawrence of Arabia.

Lowell stayed with the Victor **News** until the summer of 1912. For the fall season, he enrolled in the University of Denver. He met a young, attractive woman named Fran Ryan. But it was not until he was working on the **Chicago Evening Journal** that he decided to marry Fran.

At first, she would not agree to marry him. He was so busy traveling to Alaska, Chicago, and New York they were not able to be together for very long. Finally, in 1917, Fran and Lowell were married. They spent their honeymoon in Europe, in the midst of World War I.

The Thomas family moved from Victor in 1918. Gold production had fallen to $8,119,747 for that year. Homestake, South Dakota was the only American gold district to surpass the Cripple Creek-Victor area. But the decline of living standards in Victor was too evident. No new construction took place. Existing buildings lacked upkeep. The population had dropped to 3,000.

Victor still possessed its charisma. Too many legends had been born in the town. It would not quickly disappear from history. Although many of its structures rapidly vanished, the people who had lived in the town carried on its mystique forever in their souls. Through these people and their descendants, Victor lives on. The passing of time cannot erase the desires of the people who built the town on a mountain of gold.

Lowell Thomas wrote of Victor: "...trails now overgrown and forgotten, and forgotten with them the dreams of thousands of eager and hard-working men and women, all now gone from that place...all are a curiosity...But whenever I go back and stand a moment at Windy Point, they all come to life again."[43]

1949: Lowell Thomas arrives in Victor on the last run of the Midland Terminal. He was presented with the key to the city. Later, he and Ralph Carr (former Governor of Colorado and rival editor of the Cripple Creek Times) inspected the old Victor Daily Record building. They had found its windows boarded and a "For Sale" on the door.   Pioneer Museum

1949: the groundbreaking ceremony for the Carlton Mill. Lowell Thomas was in a familiar place--before a microphone. Lowell Thomas, Jr. is standing at the far left, one foot on the speaking platform. Mrs. A.E. Carlton is at the far right talking to Mrs. Lowell Thomas. In this same year, the Midland Terminal Railroad made its last run.   Victor/Lowell Thomas Museum

1921-1980

Between 1921 and 1926, Lowell traveled the world. In 1924, he and his wife, Fran, moved in with Dr. and Mrs. Thomas. They stayed in their home in New Jersey long enough for Lowell to write **With Lawrence in Arabia.** The book was published by The Century Company in 1924. In the past fifty years, the book has gone through over one hundred printings. The rest of 1924 was filled with an American coast-to-coast tour of the Allenby-Lawrence show.

In 1925, Lowell and Fran traveled 26,000 miles by airplane through twenty-one European countries. When they returned in the fall of 1926, they bought Clover Brook Farm in Quaker Hill, New York. Lowell signed a deal with Doubleday Publishing Company to write six books.

He found it necessary to hire a personal editor. Prosper Buranelli was the prime candidate. Buranelli, editor of Simon and Schuster's first publishing venture in 1924--**The Crossword Puzzle Book**--became one of Lowell's closest friends. Lowell constantly acquired so much work to accomplish that Buranelli often lived at Clover Brook Farm.

Buranelli helped Lowell with his books, broadcasts, talks, and films. In later years, Mary Davis was hired to head Lowell's New York office. Electra Ward and Gene Nicks aided the broadcasting of the radio shows which emanated from the studio in his home. No matter how much work he brought home, he and his staff managed to finish it successfully.

Most of the people in his organization, like Electra Ward, Prosper Buranelli, Mary Davis, Gene Nicks, Frank Smith, and Gerald Dickler stayed with Lowell for life.

6 October 1923: Lowell Thomas, Jr. was born in London. On the same day, Harry Chase introduced the Thomases to radio: he brought a "crystal set" into the hospital to entertain Fran.

21 March 1925: Lowell Thomas spoke for the first time on radio as the official historian for the first world flight. The station was KDKA in Pittsburgh. This station had first broadcasted 2 November 1920.

29 September 1930: Lowell Thomas replaced Floyd Gibbons on NBC's "Literary Digest." Lowell was the first news commentator to broadcast for both NBC and CBS. His program lasted forty-six years.

21 February 1940: Lowell Thomas was the first television news broadcaster. He did not care to stay with television for very long because it limited his freedom to travel. At the time, radio equipment was much easier and more practical to transport than television equipment.

He also had his Fox-Movietone News contract to think of, which he had signed in 1932. He adored keeping busy, but he could not work more than seven days in a week.

1946: Frank Smith joined the Thomas organization. Capitol Cities Communications was formed. Smith began buying radio and television stations, magazines and newspapers for Thomas. The **Kansas City Star,** where Ernest Hemingway began his career, became part of the Thomas organization. Also in this year, Lowell moved his world-renown voice exclusively to CBS.

1951-55 saw the rise of Cinerama, the three-dimensional movie process that delighted the world. **This Is Cinerama, Seven Wonders of the World,** and **Search for Paradise** were the only original Cinerama films. They were all made by Lowell Thomas. Fred Waller invented the process and Buzz Reeves developed it, using three projectors and a nine-speaker sound system. Lowell Thomas' Cinerama Productions Corporation wrote, directed, and produced these three innovational films.

1957-59: Lowell Thomas, Jr. produced his father's television series, **High Adventure.** Each show was given a budget of $250,000 by its sponsor, General Motors. The cannibals of the Sepik River in New Guinea were the subject of the first show.

6 January 1976: Lowell Thomas received the highest honor an American citizen can be awarded. The Medal of Freedom was presented to him by President Gerald Ford.

30 April 1976: Lowell Thomas announced in Victor, Colorado that his last broadcast would be 14 May 1976. For forty-six years, he was one of the most listened-to men in America, and possibly in the world. Lowell Thomas attributed that honor to his convenient time slot on the radio just before the **Amos'n'Andy Show.**

August 1981: Lowell Thomas (in Excalibur) tells Mrs. Thomas, Wayne McCormick (far left), and Marshall Sprague a tale of the Anaconda Mine. Marshall Sprague, long a friend of Lowell Thomas, is the author of such books as Money Mountain the story of the Cripple Creek District. McCormick is president of the association which supports the Victor/Lowell Thomas Museum.

Photo by Joanne Shideler

1981

13 August: Lowell Thomas was in Colorado Springs to speak in the "Past as Prologue" series funded by the National Endowment for the Humanities. He stayed at the Broadmoor Hotel. His rooms were filled with old friends and acquaintances. The telephone perpetually rang. He had never left the Pike's Peak Region.

After a busy day, he and his second wife, Marianna--whom he had married in January 1976, were escorted by Marshall Sprague to the Palmer High School Auditorium. Marshall Sprague, author of **Money Mountain,** had long been a friend of Lowell Thomas. Both had been newspapermen in New York. They had remained close friends long after Sprague moved to Colorado Springs.

My brother, Ross, and I had been in contact with Mr. Thomas earlier in the summer. Since June, we had been working on the Lowell Thomas Exhibit in the Victor/Lowell Thomas Museum. Even though Mr. Thomas politely expressed to us that he was not ready to be "immortalized" in a museum, he offered to help us in any way he could. On 13 August, we went to meet Mr. Thomas and confirm arrangements for his return to Victor. Of course, we were not about to miss Mr. Thomas' talk about his memories of the Cripple Creek-Victor Mining District.

Never having seen Lowell Thomas perform, I was literally amazed. Without chair or podium, Mr. Thomas stood before a full house and kept everyone entertained for two hours. The performance was too short. He told his stories masterfully, holding the audience's attention until the last word of the last anecdote. His memory was outstanding. Whether with humor or mystery, adventure or pathos, each word he emoted was cherished like a nugget of gold.

Lowell Thomas was eighty-nine years old. He captured the stage with the charismatic power of a young man bounding with energy.

17 August: we drove Lowell and Marianna Thomas up to Victor. Millions of questions had been in our minds. Few were asked. We had studied Mr. Thomas' life and career in order to reorganize the exhibit in the museum. But when we had our chance to be objective, we were too much in awe to be inquisitive.

Once in the mining district, things began to change. We drove the backroads of the area so Mr. Thomas could refamiliarize himself with his adolescent surroundings. The sights encouraged him to tell stories. We all relived the past with him.

I had studied the history and landscape of the area for over a year. I was sure I understood the district to a point where I could write about it. When Mr. Thomas opened the door which let us traverse backwards eighty years, I realized that all I knew were stark historical facts. Mr. Thomas helped me to feel the human drama of the era. He recreated the atmosphere of another time and place.

Victor was suddenly alive and breathing. No longer was it merely a page of printed history.

We had lunch at Zeke's on South Third Street in Victor. A picture of Lowell Thomas with the cannibals of the Sepik River in New Guinea hung behind the bar. Mr. Thomas had sent the picture years before. He had entitled it, "The Man Who Came To Dinner." He was at home in the rustic environment of the bar. When he looked around, he saw people and things I could not. I asked him if Victor's decline depressed him. He replied, "I never get depressed."

Victorites and vacationers gathered around our table. The attention inspired Mr. Thomas to tell more stories about the area. I was foolish not to have a tape recorder. The tales flowed as richly as the gold once did from Battle Mountain. I had been up to Victor countless times in the past to do research. But this time, I was in the town at the turn of the century.

Our entourage grew as we walked up Third Street to the Victor/Lowell Thomas Museum. Mr. Thomas wanted to see the exhibit before the dedication ceremony that night. He was delighted to talk to people whom he had met during his many return visits to Victor. Few of the people he had grown up with were still living. Even a smaller number had remained in the town. But Mr. Thomas was pleased to speak with everyone. Nearly all who saw him had met him somewhere else in the world in the last sixty years.

Ross and I were a bit worried that our exhibit would not be what Mr. Thomas expected. Our fears were soon quelled. Upon entering the exhibit, the first picture he saw suggested a tale. His entire visit to the museum soared along that route. I can still hear him saying, "Well, that reminds me of another story...."

A large, colorful five-piece poster from the 1920's advertising his "With Allenby in Palestine and Lawrence in Arabia" show made him remember the time **The Seven Wonders of the World** opened in Denver. The Cinerama movie was an astounding success. The Cooper Theater in Denver was one of the twenty-two cinemas around the world equipped to run the film. In 1953, Mr. Thomas chartered buses and took everyone in the Cripple Creek-Victor area to Denver to see the movie. Dinner was served, and then all went to the movies. Mr. Thomas picked up the bill.

A Midland Terminal register was part of the exhibit. When Mr. Thomas saw it, he remembered a trip back to Victor in 1949. His son, Lowell Thomas, Jr., had accompanied him. It was the last run of the train before it was dismantled. Ralph Carr joined the Thomas party. Carr had been governor of Colorado from 1938 to 1946. They re-explored the district, making sure they visited the sites of the Victor **Daily Record** and the Cripple Creek **Times**. Once Lowell Thomas and Ralph Carr were rival editors, but they were always friends.

Lowell Thomas, Lowell Thomas, Jr., and Ralph Carr were present at the groundbreaking ceremonies for Mrs. A.E. Carlton's new gold ore processing mill in this same year.

12 March 1951, Thomas and Carr saw each other again at the dedication ceremonies of the completed Carlton Mill. Both men spoke on the occasion. Later that day, at 4:45 P.M., Lowell Thomas performed his daily broadcast on CBS Radio from the Victor Elks Club.

Mr. Thomas could have told us entertaining stories for the rest of the day. But there was much to do in such a short time. A film crew from Colorado Springs was waiting for Mr. Thomas to speak about Victor for their cameras. Wayne "Mac" McCormick, president of the Victor/Lowell Thomas Museum, drove Mr. and Mrs. Thomas to the old City Bank Building on the northeast corner of Fourth Street and Victor Avenue in his bronze Excalibur.

As soon as the cameras were rolling, Mr. Thomas turned to Mac and said, "That reminds me, your museum used to be Tomkins Hardware and Gwillim's Confectionery...."

That night, Ross and I picked up the Thomases at the Imperial Hotel in Cripple Creek. All afternoon, Mr. Thomas had entertained news crews from Denver, Colorado Springs, Pueblo, and Canon City. On the six-mile ride back to Victor, Mr. Thomas spoke emotionally of his sisters, Pherbia and Helen. The view of Victor's Sunnyside Cemetery from the road enhanced his thoughts. The emotions were more of regret than sadness--regret that they had not been able to live longer to enjoy more of life.

When we drove up to the Victor Elks Club, once Armory Hall, none of us were prepared for the sight. Over five hundred people had congregated in front of the building awaiting the arrival of Mr. and Mrs. Thomas. When they stepped out of the car, the crowd--as if on a cue--split down the middle to form a pathway to the front door. Applause reverberated loudly in the Victor street. The sun was setting in golden streaks across the clouds. Tears of joy welled up in Lowell Thomas' blue eyes.

I knew the applause was for Mr. Thomas. But I could not help wonder if it was not also for Victor.

The town had not been so full of people for a very long time. There were only two hundred or so year-round residents at the time. The entire district's population had nearly doubled since Lowell Thomas' arrival. People had to stand in the dining hall. Every seat was taken. The inevitable occurred: Mr. Thomas was asked to speak. He quickly rose to the occasion. "Everyone knows the name Cripple Creek. History has given that town all the credit for the gold. But we all know Cripple Creek is just a suburb of Victor...."

Mr. Thomas was impressed with his visit to Victor. He decided to stay for a whole week. Camera crews followed him wherever he went. He told stories about his high school girlfriends, his jobs, the mines, the saloons, his family, the newspapers, the tenderloins--he had a tale for every step he took in Victor. He traveled 3,300 feet down the Ajax Mine to tell some stories to the miners on the day shift. When he unexpectedly came to see my brother and myself digging six feet down in an 1890's outhouse for relics of the "Old West", he exclaimed, "I've heard those old bottles are worth something. We used to throw rocks at them. Especially the ones from Cripple Creek!"

Lowell Thomas died in Pawling, New York on 29 August 1981 at home on his Hammersley Hill Estate. He had left Victor only a few days before. But he is going back.

Photograph © by Rupe Welsh.

This house on the corner of Fourth Street and Granite Avenue was the Thomas home for a short period. Located on the foot of Battle Mountain, the Gold Coin Mine, Short Line Railroad Depot, Midland Terminal Depot, most of Victor, and the Sangre de Cristos Mountain Range could be seen from the home's front windows.

The Thomas home at 227 South Sixth Street is still standing. In the late 1960's and early 1970's, the house served as the Lowell Thomas Museum in Victor. The house is now a private residence. As of late, the Victor/ Lowell Thomas Museum is located on the southeast corner of Third Street and Victor Avenue.

Helen was Lowell's first sister. Also, she was the first of the Thomases to be born in Victor. She died a little over a year after her birth. In 1904, Mrs. Thomas gave birth to Pherbia. Lowell Thomas never forgot Helen. Her grave has been well-tended in the last eighty years. Mr. Thomas felt remorseful over the fact that neither of his sisters saw as much of life as he had.

Photos by Brian Levine

NINTH ANNUAL EDITION

VICTOR DAILY RECORD

A GROUP OF THE DISTRICT'S DIVIDEND DISTRIBUTORS.

THE LEADING NEWSPAPER

OF THE

CRIPPLE CREEK DISTRICT

Tenth Year — — Thursday Morning — — March 16th 1905
— Victor, Colo. —

Peace and prosperity follow law and order. — — —

Colorado Historical Society

Footnotes

[1] Lowell Thomas, **Good Evening Everybody** (New York: William Morrow and Company, 1976), p. 29.

[2] Thomas, **Good Evening Everybody,** p. 29.

[3] Thomas, **Good Evening Everybody,** p. 49.

[4] Thomas, **Good Evening Everybody,** p. 50.

[5] Mabel Barbee Lee, **Cripple Creek Days** (Garden City: Doubleday & Company, Inc., 1958), p. 239.

[6] Lee, **Cripple Creek Days,** p. 239.

[7] Thomas, **Good Evening Everybody,** p. 31.

[8] Thomas, **Good Evening Everybody,** p. 31.

[9] Thomas, **Good Evening Everybody,** p. 32.

[10] Emma F. Langdon, **The Cripple Creek Strike** (Victor: The Press of the Victor Daily Record, 1904), p. 154.

[11] Langdon, **The Cripple Creek Strike,** p. 155.

[12] Thomas, **Good Evening Everybody,** p. 39.

[13] Thomas, **Good Evening Everybody,** p. 52.

[14] Thomas, **Good Evening Everybody,** p. 38.

[15] Thomas, **Good Evening Everybody,** p. 52.

[16] Lowell Thomas, **Beyond Khyber Pass** (New York: Century Company, 1925), p. 3.

[17] Lowell Thomas, **So Long Until Tomorrow** (New York: William Morrow and Company, Inc., 1977), p. 135.

[18] Thomas, **Good Evening Everybody,** p. 31.

[19] Lowell Thoms, **Pageant of Life** (New York: P.F. Collier & Son Corporation, 1941), p.2.

[20] Thomas, **Good Evening Everybody,** p.50.

[21] Thomas, **Good Evening Everybody,** p. 50.

[22] Thomas, **Good Evening Everybody,** p. 60.

[23] Lowell Thomas, **History As You Heard It** (Garden City: Doubleday & Company Inc., 1957), p. 1.

[24] Thomas, **Good Evening Everybody,** p. 59.

[25] Thomas, **Good Evening Everybody,** p. 59-60.

[26] Thomas, **Good Evening Everybody,** p. 109.

[27] Thomas, **Good Evening Everybody,** p. 56.

[28] Lee, **Cripple Creek Days,** p. 239.

[29] Thomas, **Good Evening Everybody,** p. 56.

[30]Thomas, **Good Evening Everybody,** p. 56.

[31]Thomas, **Good Evening Everybody,** p. 47.

[32]Thomas, **Good Evening Everybody,** p. 201.

[33]Thomas, **Good Evening Everybody,** p. 29.

[34]Thomas, **Good Evening Everybody,** p. 195.

[35]Thomas, **Good Evening Everybody,** p. 213.

[36]Thomas, **Good Evening Everybody,** p. 69.

[37]Thomas, **Good Evening Everybody,** p. 69.

[38]Thomas, **Good Evening Everybody,** p. 70.

[39]Thomas, **Good Evening Everybody,** p. 71.

[40]Thomas, **Good Evening Everybody,** p. 72.

[41]Thomas, **Good Evening Everybody,** p. 72.

[42]Thomas, **Good Evening Everybody,** p. 70.

[43]Thomas, **Good Evening Everybody,** p. 61.

*Victor **Daily Record,** 1900-1909.

Bibliography

Bowen, Norman R., editor. **Lowell Thomas: The Stranger Everyone Knows.** Garden City: Doubleday; 1968.

Holbrook, Stewart H. **The Rocky Mountain Revolution.** New York: Henry Holt and Company; 1956.

Lawrence, T.E. **Revolt in the Desert.** New York: George H. Doran Company; 1927.

Lawrence, T.E. **Seven Pillars of Wisdom.** Garden City: Doubleday, Doran & Company, Inc.; 1935.

Langdon, F. Emma. **The Cripple Creek Strike.** Victor: Press of the Victor Daily Record; 1904.

Lee, Mabel Barbee. **Cripple Creek Days.** Garden City: Doubleday & Company, Inc.; 1958.

Levine, Brian H. **Cities of Gold.** Denver: Stonehenge Books; 1981.

Morris, Edmund. **The Rise of Theodore Roosevelt.** New York: Coward, McCann & Geoghagan, Inc.; 1979.

Sprague, Marshall. **Colorado: A History.** New York: W.W. Norton & Company, Inc.; 1976.

Sprague, Marshall. **Money Mountain.** Lincoln and London: University of Nebraska Press; 1979.

Taylor, Robert Guilford. **Cripple Creek Mining District.** Palmer Lake: Filter Press; 1973.

Thomas, Lowell. **Beyond Khyber Pass.** New York: Century Company; 1925.

Thomas, Lowell. **Good Evening Everybody.** New York: William Morrow and Company, Inc.; 1976.

Thomas, Lowell. **History As You Heard It.** Garden City: Doubleday & Company, Inc.; 1957.

Thomas, Lowell. **Lowell Thomas' Book of the High Mountains.** New York: Julian Messner, Inc.; 1964.

Thomas, Lowell. **Pageant of Life.** New York: P.F. Collier & Son Corporation; 1941.

Thomas, Lowell. **Pageant of Romance.** New York: E.P. Dutton & Company, Inc.; 1943.

Thomas, Lowell. **Raiders of the Deep.** Garden City: Doubleday, Doran & Company, Inc.; 1928.

Thomas, Lowell. **Seven Wonder of the World.** Garden City: Hanover House; 1956.

Thomas, Lowell. **So Long Until Tomorrow.** New York: William Morrow and Company, Inc.; 1977.

Thomas, Lowell. **The Vital Spark.** Garden City: Doubleday & Company, Inc.; 1959.

Thomas, Lowell. **With Lawrence in Arabia.** New York: Century Company; 1924.

Thomas, Jr., Lowell. **Out of This World.** New York: Greystone Press; 1950.

Waters, Frank. **Midas of the Rockies.** Chicago: Swallow Press Inc.; 1949.

Victor **Daily Record.** Victor: Press of the Victor Daily Record; 1900-1909.

In the summer of 1981, Ross Levine (brother of the author) worked in the Victor/Lowell Thomas Museum as part of a work/study program. A medical student at Cornell, Ross had decided to make use of his summer by delving into Western history. He assisted in preparing the Lowell Thomas Exhibit for Mr. and Mrs. Thomas' visit in August 1981. He also helped to reorganize the Victor/Lowell Thomas Museum.

In this photograph, Lowell Thomas (right), Brian (center), and Ross (left) stood in front of the museum for Mrs. Thomas' camera. Victor Avenue is in the background.